Max Velmans

How Could Conscious Experiences Affect Brains?

In everyday life we take it for granted that we have conscious control of some of our actions and that the part of us that exercises control is the conscious mind. Psychosomatic medicine also assumes that the conscious mind can affect body states, and this is supported by evidence that the use of imagery, hypnosis, bio-feedback and other 'mental interventions' can be therapeutic in a variety of medical conditions. However, there is no accepted theory of mind/body interaction and this has had a detrimental effect on the acceptance of mental causation in science, philosophy and in many areas of clinical practice. Biomedical accounts typically translate the effects of mind into the effects of brain functioning, for example, explaining mind/body interactions in terms of the interconnections and reciprocal control of cortical, neuroendocrine, autonomic and immune systems. While such accounts are instructive, they are implicitly reductionist, and beg the question of how conscious experiences could have bodily effects. On the other hand, non-reductionist accounts have to cope with three problems: (1) The physical world appears causally closed, which would seem to leave no room for conscious intervention. (2) One is not conscious of one's own brain/body processing, so how could there be conscious control of such processing? (3) Conscious experiences appear to come too late to causally affect the processes to which they most obviously relate. This paper suggests a way of understanding mental causation that resolves these problems. It also suggests that 'conscious mental control' needs to be partly understood in terms of the voluntary operations of the preconscious mind, and that this allows an account of biological determinism that is compatible with experienced free will.

What Needs to be Explained

The assumption that we have a conscious mind that controls our voluntary functions and actions is taken for granted in everyday life and is deeply ingrained in our ethics, politics and legal systems. The potential effect of the mind on the body is also taken for granted in psychosomatic medicine. But *how* the conscious mind exercises its influence is not easy to understand. In principle, there are four distinct ways in which body/brain and mind/consciousness might enter into causal relationships. There might be physical causes of physical states, physical causes of mental states, mental causes of mental states, and mental causes of physical states. Establishing which forms of causation are effective in *practice* is important, not just for a deeper understanding of mind/body interactions, but also for the proper treatment of some forms of illness and disease.

Within conventional medicine, physical→physical causation is taken for granted. Consequently, the proper treatment for physical disorders is assumed to be some form of physical intervention. Psychiatry takes the efficacy of physical →mental causation for granted, along with the assumption that the proper treatment for psychological disorders may involve psychoactive drugs, neurosurgery and so on. Many forms of psychotherapy take mental→mental causation for granted, and assume that psychological disorders can be alleviated by means of 'talking cures', guided imagery, hypnosis and other forms of mental intervention. Psychosomatic medicine assumes that mental→physical causation can be effective ('psychogenesis'). Consequently, under some circumstances, a physical disorder (for example, hysterical paralysis) may require a mental (psychotherapeutic) intervention. Given the extensive evidence for *all* these causal interactions (cf. readings in Velmans, 1996a), how are we to make sense of them?

Clinical Evidence for the Causal Efficacy of Conscious Mental States

The problems posed by mental→physical causation are particularly acute, as reductionist, materialistic science generally takes it for granted that the operation of physical systems can be entirely explained in physical terms. Yet there is a large body of evidence that states of mind can affect not only subsequent states of the mind but also states of the body. For example, Barber (1984), Sheikh *et al.* (1996), and the readings in Sheikh (2001) review evidence that the use of imagery, hypnosis and biofeedback may be therapeutic in a variety of medical conditions.

Particularly puzzling is the evidence that under certain conditions, a range of *autonomic* body functions including heart rate, blood pressure, vasomotor activity, blood glucose levels, pupil dilation, electrodermal activity and immune system functioning can be influenced by conscious states. In some cases these effects are striking. Baars and McGovern (1996) for example report that,

> The global influence of consciousness is dramatized by the remarkable phenomenon of biofeedback training. There is firm evidence that *any* single neurone or *any* population of neurons can come to be voluntarily controlled by giving conscious feedback of their neural firing rates. A small needle electrode in the base of the thumb can tap into a single motor unit — a muscle fibre controlled by one motor neurone coming from the spinal cord, and a sensory fibre going back to it. When the signal from the muscle fibre is amplified and played back as a click through a loudspeaker, the subject can learn to control his or her single motor unit — one among millions — in about ten minutes. Some subjects have learned to play drumrolls on their single motor units after about thirty minutes of practice! However, if the biofeedback signal is not conscious, learning does not occur. Subliminal feedback, distraction from the feedback signal, or feedback via a *habituating* stimulus — all these cases prevent control being acquired. Since this kind of learning only works

for *conscious* biofeedback signals, it suggests again that consciousness creates global access to all parts of the nervous system (p. 75).

The most well accepted evidence for the effect of states of mind on medical outcome is undoubtedly the 'placebo effect' — well known to every medical practitioner and researcher. Simply receiving treatment, and having confidence in the therapy or therapist has itself been found to be therapeutic in many clinical situations (cf. Skrabanek and McCormick, 1989; Wall, 1996). As with other instances of apparent mind/body interaction, there are conflicting interpretations of the causal processes involved. For example, Skrabanek and McCormick (1989) claim that placebos can affect illness (how people feel) but not disease (organic disorders). That is, they accept the possibility of mental→mental causation but not of mental→physical causation.

However, Wall (1996) cites evidence that placebo treatments may produce organic changes. Hashish *et al.* (1988) for example, found that use of an impressive ultrasound machine reduced not only pain, but also jaw tightness and swelling after the extraction of wisdom teeth whether or not the machine was set to produce ultrasound. Wall also reviews evidence that placebos can remove the sensation of pain accompanying well-defined organic disorders, and not just the feelings of discomfort, anxiety and so on that may accompany it.

As McMahon and Sheikh (1989) note, the absence of an acceptable theory of mind/body interaction within philosophy and science has had a detrimental effect on the acceptance of mental causation in many areas of clinical theory and practice. Conversely, the extensive evidence for mental causation within some clinical settings forms part of the database that any adequate theory of mind/consciousness–body/brain relationships needs to explain.

Some Useful Accounts of Mental Causation

The theoretical problems posed by mental causation are nicely illustrated by studies of imagery. According to the evidence reviewed by Sheikh *et al.* (1996), imagery can be an effective tool in exercising mental control over ones own bodily states (heart rate, blood pressure, vasomotor activity and so on). It can also affect other states of mind, playing an important role in hypnosis and meditation. But, how could ephemeral images affect the spongy material of brains, and by what mechanism could conscious images affect other conscious states?

In clinical practice, the effects of imagery on brain, body and other conscious experience are often explained to patients in terms of *refocusing and redirection of attention*, linked where plausible to the operation of known biological mechanisms. For example, in their pain control induction programme, Syrjala and Abrams (1996) explain the effectiveness of imagery to patients in terms of the gate-control theory of pain:

> Even though the pain message starts in your leg, you won't feel pain unless your brain gets the pain message. The pain message moves along nerves from where the injury is located to the brain. These nerves enter the spinal cord, where they connect to other nerves, which send information up the spinal cord to the brain. The connections in the spinal cord and brain act like gates. These gates help you to not have to

pay attention to all the messages in your body all the time. For example, right now as you are listening, you do not notice the feelings in your legs, although those feelings are there if you choose to notice them. If you are walking, you might notice feelings in your legs but not in your mouth. One way we block the gates to pain is with medications. Or we can block the gates by filling them with other messages. You do this if you hit your elbow and then rub it hard. The rubbing fills the gate with other messages, and you feel less pain. You've done the same thing if you ever had a headache and you get busy doing something that takes a lot of concentration. You forget about the headache because the gates are full of other messages. Imagery is one way to fill the gate. You can choose to feel the pain if you need to, but any time you like you can fill the gate with certain thoughts and images. Our goal is to find the best gate fillers for you (p. 243).

While this account is nicely judged in terms of its practical value to patients, it does not give much detail about the actual mechanisms involved. Nor does it serve as a general account of mental causation in situations that seem to demand a more sophisticated understanding of the intricate, reciprocal balance of mind/brain/body relationships. The evidence that involuntary processes can sometimes be brought under voluntary control, for example, appears to blur the classical boundary between voluntary and autonomic nervous system functions, and extends the potential scope of top-down processing in the brain. Also, the evidence that imagery can sometimes have bodily effects that resemble the effects of the imaged situations themselves suggest that the conventional, clear distinction between 'psychological reality' and 'physical reality' may not be so clear in the way that these are *responded to* by body and brain. As Kenneth Pelletier (1993) puts it:

Asthmatics sneeze at plastic flowers. People with a terminal illness stay alive until after a significant event, apparently willing themselves to live until a graduation ceremony, a birthday milestone, or a religious holiday. A bout of rage precipitates a sudden, fatal heart attack. Specially trained people can voluntarily control such 'involuntary' bodily functions as the electrical activity of the brain, heart rate, bleeding, and even the body's response to infection. Mind and body are inextricably linked, and their second-by-second interaction exerts a profound influence upon health and illness, life and death. Attitudes, beliefs, and emotional states ranging from love and compassion to fear and anger can trigger chain reactions that affect blood chemistry, heart rate, and the activity of every cell and organ system in the body — from the stomach and gastrointestinal tract to the immune system. All of that is now indisputable fact. However, there is still great debate over the extent to which the mind can influence the body and the precise nature of that linkage. (p. 19)

One productive route to a deeper understanding of such linkages is the traditional biomedical one, involving a fuller understanding of the interconnections and reciprocal control between cortical, neuroendocrine, autonomic and immune systems. These have been extensively investigated within psychoneuroimmunology. Following a detailed review of this research, Watkins (1997) concludes that

It is apparent that the immune system can no longer be thought of as autoregulatory. Virtually every aspect of immune function can be modulated by the autonomic nervous system and centrally produced neuropeptides. These efferent neuro-immuno modulatory pathways are themselves modulated by afferent inputs from the immune system, the cortex and the limbic emotional centers. Thus the brain and the immune system communicate in a complex bidirectional flow of cytokines, steroids and neuropeptides, sharing information and regulating each other's function. This enables the two systems to respond in an integrated manner to environmental challenges, be they immunological or behavioral, and thereby maintain homeostatic balance (p. 15).

So Why Does Mental Causation Remain a Problem?

Such innovative findings and their practical consequences for the development of 'mind–body medicine' demand careful investigation. It is important to note however that such explanatory accounts routinely translate *mind*–body interactions into *brain*–body interactions. Unless one is prepared to accept that mind and consciousness are *nothing more* than brain processes[1] this finesses the classical mind/body problems that are *already* posed by *normal* voluntary, 'mental' control. How imagery might affect autonomic or immune system functioning is mysterious, but how a conscious wish to lift a finger makes that finger move is equally mysterious. Why? There are many reasons, but I will focus on just three.

1. The physical world appears causally closed

As noted above, it is widely accepted in science that the operation of physical systems can be entirely explained in physical terms. For example, if one examines the human brain from an external third-person perspective one can, in principle, trace the effects of input stimuli on the central nervous system all the way from input to output, without finding any 'gaps' in the chain of causation that consciousness might fill. Indeed, the *neural correlates* of consciousness would fill any 'gaps' that might potentially be filled by consciousness in the activities of brain. In any case, if one inspects the operation of the brain from the outside, no subjective experience can be observed at work. Nor does one need to appeal to the existence of subjective experience to account for the neural activity that one *can* observe. The same is true if one thinks of the brain as a functioning system described in information processing terms rather than neural terms. Once the processing within a system required to perform a given function is sufficiently well specified in procedural terms, one does not have to add an 'inner conscious life' to make the system work. In principle, the same function, operating to the same specification, could be performed by a non-conscious machine.[2]

---

[1] Although variants of eliminative/reductive physicalism and functionalism (that consciousness is nothing more than a state or function of the brain) are commonly adopted in current philosophy and science, the reduction of conscious phenomenology to brain states or functions faces well-recognized difficulties. I present a detailed analysis of the strengths and weaknesses of various eliminative, reductive and emergent forms of physicalism, along with psychofunctionalism (functionalism in cognitive psychology) and computational functionalism (functionalism in philosophy and AI) in Velmans (2000) chs. 3, 4 and 5. On-line papers addressing many of the difficulties, for example in the work of Searle, Dennett, Armstrong, Block and Tye are also available from the CogPrints archive (http://cogprints.soton.ac.uk/) — see Velmans (1998; 2001a,b). Given the current prevalence of physicalism I also summarize some of my reasons for not adopting it in the Appendix below.

[2] Note that being physically closed does not preclude 'downward causation'. Higher order brain states or functions may for example constrain lower order brain states and functions, for example in the way

2. One is not conscious of one's own brain/body processing, so how could there be conscious control of such processing?

How 'conscious' is conscious, voluntary control? It is surprising how few people bother to ask.[3] One might be aware of the fact *that* relaxing imagery can lower heart rate, but one has no awareness of *how* it does so, nor, in biofeedback, does one have any awareness of how consciousness might control the firing of a single motor neurone. One isn't even conscious of *how* to control the articulatory system in everyday 'conscious speech'! Speech production is one of the most complex tasks humans are able to perform. Yet, one has no awareness whatsoever of the motor commands issued from the central nervous system that travel down efferent fibres to innervate the muscles, nor of the complex motor programming that enables muscular co-ordination and control. In speech, for example, the tongue may make as many as twelve adjustments of shape per second — adjustments which need to be precisely coordinated with other rapid, dynamic changes within the articulatory system. According to Lenneberg (1967), within one minute of discourse as many as ten to fifteen thousand neuromuscular events occur. Yet only the *results* of this activity (the overt speech) normally enters consciousness.

Preconscious speech control might of course be the result of *prior* conscious activity, for example, planning *what* to say might be conscious, particularly if one is expressing some new idea, or expressing some old idea in a novel way. Speech production is commonly thought to involve hierarchically arranged, semantic, syntactic and motor control systems in which communicative intentions are translated into overt speech in a largely top-down fashion. Planning *what* to say and translating nonverbal conceptual content into linguistic forms requires effort. But to what extent is such planning conscious? Let us see.

A number of theorists have observed that periods of conceptual, semantic and syntactic planning are characterized by gaps in the otherwise relatively continuous stream of speech (Goldman-Eisler, 1968; Boomer, 1970). The neurologist John Hughlings Jackson, for example, suggested that the amount of planning required depends on whether the speech is 'new' speech or 'old' speech. Old speech (well-known phrases, etc.) requires little planning and is relatively continuous. New speech (saying things in a new way) requires planning and is characterized by hesitation pauses. Fodor *et al.* (1974) point out that breathing pauses also occur (gaps in the speech stream caused by the intake of breath). However, breathing pauses do not generally coincide with hesitation pauses.

Breathing pauses nearly always occur at the beginnings and ends of major linguistic constituents (such as clauses and sentences). So these appear to be coordinated with the syntactic organization of such constituents into a clausal or sentential structure. Such organization is largely automatic and preconscious. By contrast, hesitation pauses tend to occur within clauses and sentences and appear

---

that computer software constrains and controls the switching in the hardware of the machine. The software, like the higher order functioning of the brain is best described in functional terms (e.g. as an information processing system), but this does not alter the fact that the software is entirely embodied in the physical hardware, and exercises its causal effects through its embodiment in that hardware.

[3]   See the initial discussion of this issue in Velmans (1991a).

to be associated with the formulation of ideas, deciding which words best express one's meaning, and so on. If this analysis is correct, conscious planning of *what* to say should be evident during hesitation pauses — and a little examination of what one experiences during a hesitation pause should settle the matter. Try it. During a hesitation pause one might experience a certain sense of effort (perhaps the effort to put something in an appropriate way). But nothing is revealed of the *processes* that formulate ideas, translate these into a form suitable for expression in language, search for and retrieve words from memory, or assess which words are most appropriate. In short, no more is revealed of conceptual or semantic planning in hesitation pauses than is revealed of syntactic planning in breathing pauses. The fact that a process demands processing *effort* does not ensure that it is *conscious*. Indeed, there is a sense in which one is only conscious of what one wants to say *after one has said it*!

It is particularly surprising that the same may be said of *conscious verbal thoughts*. That is, the same situation applies if one formulates one's thoughts into 'covert speech' through the use of phonemic imagery, prior to its overt expression. Once one *has* a conscious verbal thought, manifested in experience in the form of phonemic imagery, the complex cognitive processes required to generate that thought, including the processing required to encode it into phonemic imagery *have already operated*. In short, covert speech and overt speech have a similar relation to the planning processes that produce them. In neither case are the complex antecedent processes available to introspection. It should be clear that this applies equally to the processes that generate the detailed spatial arrangement, colours, shapes, sizes, movements and accompanying sounds and smells of an imaged visual scene.

3. Conscious experiences appear to come too late to causally affect the processes to which they most obviously relate

In the production of overt speech and covert speech (verbal thoughts) the conscious experience that we normally associate with such processing *follows* the processing to which it relates. Given this, in what *sense* are these 'conscious processes' conscious? The same question can be asked of that most basic of conscious voluntary processes, *conscious volition itself*.

It has been known for some time that voluntary acts are preceded by a slow negative shift in electrical potential (recorded at the scalp) known as the 'readiness potential', and that this shift can precede the act by up to one second or more (Kornhuber and Deeke, 1965). In itself, this says nothing about the relation of the readiness potential to the *experienced wish* to perform an act. To address this, Libet (1985) asked subjects to note the instant they experienced a wish to perform a specified act (a simple flexion of the wrist or fingers) by relating the onset of the experienced wish to the spatial position of a revolving spot on a cathode ray oscilloscope, which swept the periphery of the face like the sweep-second hand of a clock. Recorded in this way, the readiness potential preceded the voluntary act by around 550 milliseconds, and preceded the experienced wish (to flex the wrist or fingers) by around 350 milliseconds (for spontaneous acts involving

10 M. VELMANS

no preplanning). This suggests that, like the act itself, the experienced wish (to flex one's wrist) may be one output from the (prior) cerebral processes that actually select a given response. If so, 'conscious volition' may be no more necessary for such a (preconscious) choice than the consciousness of one's own speech is necessary for its production.[4] The same is likely to apply to more complex voluntary acts, such as the voluntary control of autonomic functions through imagery and biofeedback discussed above.[5]

The Current Theoretical Impasse

As noted, there is extensive experimental and clinical evidence that conscious experiences can affect brain/body processes, and the importance of conscious experience is rightly taken for granted in everyday life. In one sense this can be explained by a more sophisticated biomedical understanding of mind/brain/body relationships. But in a deeper sense, current attempts to understand the role of conscious experience face an impasse. How can experiences have a causal influence on a physical world that is causally closed? How can one consciously control something that one is not conscious of? How can experiences affect processes that *precede* them? Dualist-interactionist accounts of the consciousness–brain relationship, in which an autonomously existing consciousness influences the brain, do not even recognize these 'how' problems let alone address them. Materialist reductionists attempt to finesse such problems by challenging the accuracy, causal efficacy and even the existence of conscious experiences. This evades the need to address the 'how' questions, but denies the validity of the clinical evidence and defies common sense. I have given a detailed critique of the many variants of dualism and reductionism elsewhere and will not repeat it here.[6] In what follows I suggest a way through the impasse that is neither dualist nor reductionist.[7]

Ontological Monism Combined with Epistemological Dualism

How can one reconcile the evidence that conscious experiences are causally effective with the principle that the physical world is causally closed? One

[4] As Libet observed, the experienced wish *follows* the readiness potential, but *precedes* the motor act itself (by around 200 msec) — time enough to consciously *veto* the wish before executing the act. In a manner reminiscent of the interplay between the libidinous desires arising from Freud's unconscious *id* and the control exercised by the conscious *ego*, Libet suggested that the *initiation* of voluntary act and the accompanying wish are developed preconsciously, but consciousness can then act as a form of censor which decides whether or not to carry out the act. While this is an interesting possibility, it does invite an obvious question. If the wish to perform an act is developed preconsciously, why doesn't the decision to censor the act have its own preconscious antecedents? Libet (1996) argues that it *might* not need to do so as voluntary control imposes a change on a wish that is already conscious. Yet, it seems very odd that a wish to do something has preconscious antecedents while a wish not to do something does not. As it happens, there is evidence that bears directly on this issue. Karrer *et al.* (1978), and Konttinen and Lyytinen (1993), for example, found that *refraining* from irrelevant movements is associated with a slow *positive-going* readiness potential.

[5] This could be tested using Libet's procedures, by examining the relation of the readiness potential to an experienced wish to control a given bodily function via imagery or biofeedback.

[6] See Velmans (2000) chs. 2, 3, 4 and 5 and the Appendix below.

[7] In the space available I can give only an introduction to how one might resolve these problems. A more detailed treatment is given in Velmans (2000) ch. 11.

simple way is to accept that for each individual there is *one* 'mental life' but *two* ways of knowing it: first-person knowledge and third-person knowledge. From a first-person perspective conscious experiences appear causally effective. From a third-person perspective the same causal sequences can be explained in neural terms. It is not the case that the view from one perspective is right and the other wrong. These perspectives are complementary. The differences between how things appear from a first- versus a third-person perspective has to do with differences in the *observational arrangements* (the means by which a subject and an external observer access the subject's mental processes).

Let's see how this might work in practice. Suppose you have a calming image of lying in a green field on a summer's day, and you can feel the difference this makes in producing a relaxed state, slowing your breathing, removing the tension in your body and so on. You give a causal account of what is going on, based on what you experience. From my external observer's perspective, I can also observe what is going on — but what I observe is a little different. I can measure the effects on your breathing and muscle tension, but no matter how closely I inspect your brain I cannot observe your experienced image. The closest I can get to it are its neural correlates in the visual system, association areas and so on.[8] Nevertheless, if I could observe all the neurophysiological events operating in your brain to produce your relaxed bodily state, I could give a complete, physical account of what is going on. So, now you have a first-person account of what is going on that makes sense to you and I have a third-person account of what is going on that makes sense to me. How do these relate? To understand this we need to examine the relation of your visual image to its neural correlates with care.

The neural correlates of conscious experience

Although we know little about the physical nature of the neural correlates of conscious experiences, there are three plausible, functional constraints imposed by the phenomenology of consciousness itself. Normal human conscious experiences are representational (phenomenal consciousness is always *of* something).[9]

---

[8]   The neural correlates of a given experience accompany or *co-occur* with given experiences, and are by definition as close as one get to those experiences from an external observer's perspective. This differentiates them from the antecedent causes (such as the operation of selective attention, binding, etc.) which may be thought of as the necessary and sufficient *prior* conditions for given experiences in the human brain.

[9]   My assumption that normal conscious experiences are representational is driven by a Critical Realist epistemology (developed in Velmans, 2000, ch. 7) and not by any commitment to the view that mental states are nothing more than computations on representations (a thesis that is currently in dispute). While I do not have space to develop the case for Critical Realism here, it is worth noting that there is nothing mysterious about experiences being representations of entities and events outside or within our bodies and brains that differ in some respects from the alternative representations of those entities and events given by science (e.g. by physics). Perceptual processes are likely to have developed in response to evolutionary pressures, and select, attend to and interpret information in accordance with human adaptive needs. Consequently, they only need to model a subset of the available information. At the same time our perceptual models must be useful, otherwise it is unlikely that human beings would have survived. Given this, it seems reasonable to assume that, barring illusions or hallucinations, the experiences produced by perceptual processing are partial, approximate but nonetheless useful representations of what is 'really there'. *[footnote continued over page]*

Given this, it is reasonable to assume that the neural correlates of such experiences are also representational states.

Although this assumption has not always been made explicit in theories of consciousness it is largely taken for granted in psychological theory. Psychophysics, for example, takes it for granted that for any discriminable aspect of experience (a just noticeable change in brightness, colour, pitch and so on) there will be a correlated change in some state of the brain. It follows from this that the information encoded in experience (in terms of discriminable differences) will also be encoded in the brain. The same is true for the more còmplex contents of consciousness, in the many cognitive theories that associate (or identify) such contents with information stored in primary (working) memory, information at the focus of attention, information in a global workspace and so on.

A representational state must, of course, represent *something*, that is it must have a given content. For a given physical state to be the correlate of a given experience it is plausible to assume that it represents the *same* thing (otherwise it would not be the correlate of *that* experience).

Finally, for a physical state to be the correlate of a given experience, it is reasonable to suppose that it has the same 'grain'. That is, for every discriminable attribute of experience there will be a distinct, correlated, physical state. As each experience and its physical correlate represents the same thing it follows that each experience and its physical correlate encodes the same information about that thing. That is, they are representations with the same *information structure*.[10, 11]

The view that some conscious experiences are representational in the sense of being 'intentional' (that they are *of* something) has in any case been widely accepted in philosophy of mind since Brentano reintroduced this medieval notion in the nineteenth century. According to some philosophers not all conscious experiences are intentional. Searle (1994b) for example maintains that 'a feeling of pain or a sudden sense of anxiety, where there is no object of the anxiety, are not intentional' (p. 380). In Velmans (1990; 2000) I argue that a conscious experience does not have to be about a specific external object for it to be representational. It may for example represent a state of one's own body or it may represent a global *reaction* to a real, imagined or remembered event. A feeling of pain, for example, represents (in one's first-person experience) actual or potential damage to the body, and it is usually quite accurate in that it is normally subjectively located at or near the site of body damage. A feeling of anxiety is a first-person representation of a state of one's own body and brain that signals actual or potential danger, and so on. Viewed this way, *all* conscious states are about something. On this issue, I adopt the same stance as that developed by Tye (1995).

[10] This assumption of conscious experience/neural correlate functional equivalence (defined in information processing terms) is a point of convergence between otherwise widely divergent theories (physicalism, functionalism, dual-aspect theory). As Gardner (1987) points out, the assumption that mental processes operate on representations lies at the foundation of cognitive science. However, the claim that the neural correlates of conscious states are representations begs no questions about the forms that these representations might take, or about how mental processes operate on them. Representations might be iconic, propositional, feature sets, prototypes, procedural, localized, distributed, static or dynamic, or whatever. Operations might be formal and computational, or more like the patterns of shifting weights and probabilities that determine the activation patterns in neural networks. I suggest that the correlates of consciousness represent what the phenomenology itself represents, irrespective of how the correlates embody those representations.

[11] This approach has its origins in Spinoza's dual-aspect theory, which I developed into a naturalized, dual-aspect theory of information in Velmans (1991a,b; 1993; 1996; 2000). This dual-aspect theory of information also has similarities to that adopted by Chalmers (1996) (see Velmans, 2000, p. 281, note 5, for a summary of both the similarities and differences). Note that having an identical referent

If these assumptions are well founded, your experience and the neural correlates that I observe will relate to each other in a very precise way. What you experience takes the form of visual or other imagery accompanied by feelings about lying on the grass on a summery day. What I observe *is the same information* (about the visual scene) encoded in the physical correlates of what you experience in your brain. The information structure of what you and I observe is identical, although it is displayed or 'formatted' in very different ways. From your point of view, the only information you have about your own state of mind is the imagery and accompanying feelings that you experience. From my point of view, the only information you have (about your own state of mind) is the information I can see encoded in your brain. The way your information (about your own state) is displayed appears to be very different to you and me for the reason that the 'observational arrangements' by which we access that information are entirely different. From my external, third-person perspective I can only access the information encoded in your mind/brain by means of my visual or other exteroceptive systems aided by appropriate equipment. With these means I can detect the information displayed in the form of neural encodings, but not in the form of accompanying experiences. While you maintain your focus on the imaged scene, you cannot observe its neural correlates in your own brain (you would need to use my equipment for that). Nevertheless, the information in those correlates displays 'naturally',[12] in the form of the imaged scene that you experience.

But what is your mind *really* like? From my 'external observer's perspective', can I assume that what you experience is really nothing more than the physical correlates that I can observe? From my external perspective, do I know what is going on in your mind/brain/consciousness better than you do? No. I know something about your mental states that you do not know (their physical embodiment). But you know something about them that I do not know (their manifestation in your experience). Such first- and third-person information is *complementary.* We need your first-person story and my third-person story for a complete account of what is going on. If so, the nature of the mind is revealed as much by how it appears from one perspective as the other. It is not *either* physical *or* conscious experience, it is at once physical *and* conscious experience (depending on the observational arrangements). For lack of a better term we may describe this nature as *psychophysical.*[13, 14] If we combine this with the representational features above,

and information structure does not mean that experiences are *nothing more than* their neural correlates (as eliminativists and reductionists assume). A filmed version of the play *Hamlet*, recorded on videotape, for example, may have the same sequential information structure as the same play displayed in the form of successive, moving pictures on a TV screen. But it is obvious that the information on the videotape is not ontologically identical to the information displayed on the screen. In this instance, the same information is embodied in two different ways (patterns of magnetic variation on tape versus patterns of brightness and hue in individual pixels on screen) and it is displayed or 'formatted' in two different ways (only the latter display is in visible form).

[12] I assume it to be a *natural* fact about the world that certain forms of neural activity are accompanied by conscious experiences. Consequently, when such neural activities (the correlates) occur in one's brain one has the corresponding experiences. I also assume that the formatting of neurally encoded

we can say that mind is a psychophysical process that encodes information, developing over time.

An Initial Way to Make Sense of the Causal Interactions between Consciousness and Brain

This brief analysis of how first- and third-person accounts relate to each other can be used to make sense of the different *forms* of causal interaction that are taken for granted in everyday life or suggested in the clinical and scientific literature. Physical→physical causal accounts describe events from an entirely third-person perspective (they are 'pure third-person accounts'). Mental→mental causal accounts describe events entirely from a first-person perspective (they are 'pure first-person accounts'). Physical→mental and mental→physical causal accounts are mixed-perspective accounts employing perspectival switching

---

information relates to the formatting of corresponding, phenomenally encoded information in an orderly way, with discoverable neural-state space/phenomenal space mappings. An obvious example would be the way that information about spatial location and extension encoded in the brain is mapped into the 3D phenomenal space that we ordinarily experience. In vision, some progress has already been made in the discovery of such mappings (see the Special Issue on the work of Roger Shepard in *Behavioural and Brain Sciences*, **24** (4), 2001). While neural state/phenomenal state mappings are likely to differ in different sense modalities (e.g. vision versus audition) and even between different features of a given modality (e.g. colour versus spatial location and extension) there may also be shared, underlying principles (cf. Stoffregen and Benoît, 2001).

[13] The struggle to find a model or even a form of words that somehow captures the dual-aspect nature of mind is reminiscent for example of wave-particle complementarity in quantum mechanics — although this analogy is far from exact. Light either appears to behave as electromagnetic waves or as photon particles depending on the observation arrangements. It does not make sense to claim that electromagnetic waves really *are* particles (or vice versa). A complete understanding of light requires both complementary descriptions — with consequent struggles to find an appropriate way of characterizing the nature of light and other QM phenomena which encompass both descriptions ('wave-packets', 'electron clouds' and so on). This has not prevented physics from developing very precise accounts of light viewed *either* as waves *or* as particles, together with precise formulae for relating wave-like properties (such as electromagnetic frequency) to particle-like ones (such as photon energy). If first- and third-person accounts of consciousness and its physical correlates are complementary and mutually irreducible, an analogous 'psychological complementarity principle' might be required to understand the nature of mind. A more detailed discussion of how psychological complementarity relates to physical complementarity is given in Velmans (2000) ch. 11, note 19.

[14] At the macrocosmic level, the relation of electricity to magnetism also provides a clear parallel to the form of dual-aspect theory I have in mind. If one moves a wire through a magnetic field this produces an electrical current in the wire. Conversely, if one passes an electrical current through a wire this produces a surrounding magnetic field. But it does not make sense to suggest that the current in the wire is nothing more than the surrounding magnetic field, or vice-versa (reductionism). Nor is it accurate to suggest that electricity and magnetism are energies of entirely different kinds that happen to interact (dualist-interactionism). Rather these are two manifestations (or 'dual-aspects') of *electromagnetism*, a more fundamental energy that grounds and unifies both, described with elegance by Maxwell's Laws. Analogously, phenomenally encoded information and its correlated neurally encoded information may be two manifestations (or 'dual-aspects') of a more fundamental, psychophysical mind, and their relationship may, in time, be describable by neurophenomenological laws (see also note 12, above). It goes without saying that a *fully* satisfying psychophysical account of any given mental state would have to specify how given complementary first- and third-person descriptions relate to each with precision (perhaps with the elegance of Maxwell's Laws). However, such empirical relationships can only be discovered by neuropsychological research, and for the present I am only concerned with the *form* that causal accounts based on such research might need to take to resolve this aspect of the 'causal paradox'.

(Velmans, 1996b). Such accounts start with a description of causes viewed from one perspective (either first- or third-person) and then switch to a description of effects viewed from the other perspective. To understand such accounts one first has to acknowledge that a perspectival switch has taken place.

Physical→mental causal accounts start with events viewed from a third-person perspective and switch to how things appear from a first-person perspective. For example, a causal account of visual perception starts with a third-person description of the physical stimulus and the visual system but then switches to a first-person account of what the subject experiences. Mental→physical causal accounts switch the other way. From your subjective point of view, for example, the imagery that you experience is causing your heart rate to slow down and your body to relax (effects that I can measure). If I could identify the exact neural correlates of what you experience, it might be possible for me to give an entirely third-person account of this sequence of events (in terms of higher order neural representations having top-down effects on other brain and body states). But the mixed-perspective account actually gives you a more immediately useful description of what is going on in terms of the things that you can do (maintain that state of mind, deepen it, alter it, and so on).

In principle, complementary first- and third-person sources of information can be found whenever body or mind/brain states are represented in some way in subjective experience. A patient might for example have insight into the nature of a psychological problem (via feelings and thoughts), that a clinician might investigate by observing his/her brain or behaviour. In medical diagnosis, a patient might have access to some malfunction via interoceptors, producing symptoms such as pain and discomfort, whereas a doctor might be able to identify the cause via his/her exteroceptors (eyes, ears and so on) supplemented by medical instrumentation. As with conscious states and their neural correlates the clinician has access to the physical embodiment of such conditions, while the patient has access to how such conditions are experienced. In these situations, neither the third-person information available to the clinician nor the first-person information available to the patient is *automatically* privileged or 'objective' in the sense of being 'observer-free'. The clinician merely reports what he/she observes or infers about what is going on (using available means) and the patient does likewise. Such first- and third-person accounts of the subject's mental life or body states are complementary, and mutually irreducible. *Taken together*, they provide a global, psychophysical picture of the condition under scrutiny.

Conscious Experiences are Current, Global Representations Formed by the Mind/Brain

The above, I hope, gives an initial indication of how one can reconcile the evidence that conscious experiences appear causally effective with the principle that the physical world is causally closed. But there are two further, equally perplexing problems. (1) How can conscious experiences be causally effective if they come too late to affect the mind/brain processes to which they most obviously relate? (2) How can the contents of consciousness affect brain and body states when one is not conscious of the biological processes that govern those states?

I suggest that to make sense of these puzzles, one has to begin by accepting the facts rather than sweeping them under some obscuring theoretical carpet. Why do experiences come too late to affect the mind/brain processes to which they most closely relate? For the simple reason that experiences relate most closely to the processes that *produce* them. Visual perception becomes 'conscious' once visual processing results in a conscious visual experience, cognitive processing becomes 'conscious' once it produces the inner speech that forms a conscious thought and so on. Once such experiences arise the processes that have produced them have already taken place. Given this, what is consciousness actually contributing to conscious perception, to conscious speech, to conscious thought, to conscious voluntary control, and so on?[15]

As noted above, I am proceeding on the assumption that conscious experiences are representations. Some experiences represent states of the external world (exteroceptive experiences), some represent states of the body (interoceptive experiences), and some represent states of the mind/brain itself (volitions, thoughts about thoughts, etc.). Experiences can also represent past, future, real and imaginary events, for example in the form of thoughts and images.

Whatever their representational content, current experiences also tell one something important about the current state of one's own mind/brain — that it currently has percepts, feelings, thoughts, images, etc., of a given type, and that it has formed current representations with that particular content, as opposed to any

---

[15] In Velmans (1991) I argue that there are three distinct senses in which a process may be said to be conscious. It can be conscious (a) in the sense that one is conscious *of* it, (b) in the sense that it *results* in a conscious experience, and (c) in the sense that consciousness *causally affects* that process. We do not have introspective access to how the preconscious cognitive processes that enable thinking produce individual, conscious thoughts in the form of 'inner speech'. However, the content of such thoughts and the sequence in which they appear does give some insight into the way the cognitive processes (of which they are manifestations) operate over time in problem solving, thinking, planning and so on. Consequently such cognitive processes are partly conscious in sense (a), but only insofar as their detailed operation is made explicit in conscious thoughts, thereby becoming accessible to introspection. Many psychological processes are conscious in sense (b), but not in sense (a) — that is, we are not conscious of how they operate, but we are conscious of their *results*. This applies to perception in all sense modalities. When consciously reading this sentence, for example, you become aware of the printed text on the page, accompanied, perhaps, by inner speech (phonemic imagery) and a feeling of understanding (or not), but you have no introspective access to the processes which enable you to read. Nor does one have introspective access to the *details* of most other forms of cognitive functioning, for example to the detailed operations which enable 'conscious' learning, remembering, engaging in conversations with others and so on.

Crucially, having an experience that gives some introspective access to a given process, or having the results of that process manifest in an experience, says nothing about whether that experience *carries out* that process. Whether a process is 'conscious' in sense (a) or (b) needs to distinguished from whether it is conscious in sense (c). Indeed, it is not easy to envisage how the experience that makes a process conscious in sense (a) or (b), *could* make it conscious in sense (c). Consciousness *of* a physical process does not make consciousness responsible for the operation of that process (watching a kettle does not determine when it comes to the boil). So, how could consciousness *of* a mental process carry out the functions of that process? Alternatively, if conscious experience *results* from a mental process it arrives *too late* to carry out the functions of that process (see Velmans, 2000, ch. 9 for a more detailed discussion).

others. For example, the thoughts that enter consciousness at a given moment 'represent' the current state of one's own cognitive system in that they reveal *which* of many possible cognitions are currently at the focus of attention in a reportable form. If your thoughts are conscious, and I ask you what you are thinking about, you can tell me. Likewise, your visually imaged peaceful world and your conscious feelings about it represent a current, voluntarily produced representational state (and affective responses to it) within your own visual, cognitive and affective systems — and if I want to know what that is like, you can tell me.

Why don't we have more detailed experiences of the processes which produce such conscious experiences, or of the detailed workings of our own bodies, minds and brains? Because for normal purposes we don't need them! Our primary need is to interact successfully with the external world and with each other — and for that, the processes by which we arrive at representations of ourselves in the world, or which govern the many internal, adaptive adjustments we have to make are best left on 'automatic'. This is exemplified by the well-accepted transition of skills from being conscious to being nonconscious as they become well learnt (as in reading or driving a car). The global representations that we have of ourselves in the world nevertheless provide a useful, reasonably accurate representation of what is going on.[16]

How to Make Sense of the Causal Role of the Contents of Consciousness

As noted above, normal experiences are *of* something, i.e. they represent entities, events and processes in the external world, the body and the mind/brain itself. In everyday life we also behave as 'naïve realists'. That is we take the events we experience to *be* the events that are actually taking place, although sciences such as physics, biology and psychology might represent the same events in very different ways. For everyday purposes, the assumption that the world just *is* as we experience it to be serves us well. When playing billiards, for example, it is safe to assume that the balls are smooth, spherical, coloured, and cause each other to move by mechanical impact. One only has to judge the precise angle at which the white ball hits the red ball to pocket the red. A quantum mechanical description of the microstructure of the balls or of the forces they exert on each other won't improve one's game.

That said, the experienced world is not the world *in itself* — and it is not our experience *of* the balls that governs the movement of the balls themselves. Balls as-experienced and their perceived interactions are global *representations* of autonomously existing entities and their interactions, and conscious representations of such entities or events can only be formed once they exist, or after they have taken place. The same may be said of the events and processes that we experience to occur in our own bodies or minds/brains. When we withdraw a

---

[16] It is reasonable to suppose that the detail of conscious representation has been tailored by evolutionary pressures to be useful for everyday human activities (although these remain global, approximate and species-specific). To obtain a more intricate knowledge of the external world, body or mind/brain we usually need the assistance of scientific instruments. A much fuller analysis of these points is given in Velmans (2000), ch. 7.

hand quickly from a hot iron we experience the pain (in the hand) to cause what we do, but the reflex action actually takes place before the experience of pain has time to form. This can also happen with voluntary movements. Suppose, for example, that you are required to press a button as soon as you feel a tactile stimulus applied to your skin. A typical reaction time is 100 ms or so. It takes only a few milliseconds for the skin stimulus to reach the cortical surface, but Libet, *et al*. (1979) found that awareness of the stimulus takes at least 200 ms to develop. If so, the reaction must take place preconsciously, although we *experience* ourselves as responding *after* we feel something touching the skin. The mind/brain requires time to form a conscious representation of a pain or of something touching the skin and of the subsequent response. Although the conscious representations accurately place the cause (the stimulus) before the effect (the response), once the representations are formed, both the stimulus and the response have already taken place.[17]

Just as the interactions amongst experienced billiard balls represent causal sequences in the external world, but are not the events themselves, experienced interactions between our sensations, thoughts, images and actions represent causal sequences within our bodies and brains, but are not the events themselves. The thoughts, images and feelings that appear in our awareness are both *generated by* processes in our bodies and mind/brains and *represent* the current states of those processes. Thoughts and images represent the ongoing state of play of our cognitive systems; feelings represent our internal (positive and negative) reactions to and judgments about events (see Mangan, 1993, and the discussion above).

In sum, conscious representations of inner, body and external events are not the events themselves, but they generally represent those events and their causal interactions sufficiently well to allow a fairly accurate understanding of what is happening in our lives. Although they are only *representations* of events and their causal interactions, for everyday purposes we can take them to *be* those events and their causal interactions. When we play billiards we can line up a shot without the assistance of physics. Although our knowledge of our own inner states is not incorrigible, when we experience our verbal thoughts expressed in covert or overt speech, we usually know all we need to know about what we currently think — without the assistance of cognitive psychology. When we experience ourselves to have acted out of love or fear, we usually have an adequate understanding of our motivation — although a neuropsychologist might find it

---

[17] Although conscious experiences arise too late to play a causal role in the processes with which they are most closely associated (those that produce them), once they arise, they are not, of course, too late to play a causal role in other, *subsequent* mind/brain/body states or activities. A pain in the tooth, for example, might persist long enough to force one to the dentist. A desire for employment might lead one to make a job application and so on. However such forms of mental"physical causation still face the problem (already discussed) that the physical world is causally closed. For example, the physical movements that take one to the dentist can be explained by the way that the neural correlates of the pain enter into the control of motor systems, the desire for employment in terms of a goal state that is represented in one's CNS and so on. Such forms of mental causation can, however, be understood as 'mixed-perspective' causal accounts of the kind described above. See also the extensive treatment of this particular issue in discussion with Rakover (1996) in Velmans (1996b).

useful to give a third-person account of emotion in terms of its neural substrates in the neocortical, subcortical, diencephalic, midbrain and pontine-medullary brainstem systems (Watt, 2000). When we image ourselves in green grass on a summer's day and feel relaxed we are usually right to assume that the mental state that is represented in our imagery has produced a real bodily effect. For everyday life, it doesn't matter that we don't understand how such imaged scenarios are constructed by preconscious mental processes or exercise top-down control in the mind/brain/body system. It is not the case that a lower level (microscopic) representation is always better than a macroscopic one (in the case of billiard balls). Nor are third-person accounts always better than first-person ones (in describing or attempting to control our thoughts, images and emotions). The value of a given representation, description or explanation can only be assessed in the light of the purposes for which it is to be used.

Who's in Control?

The difference between voluntary and involuntary bodily functions is accepted wisdom, enshrined in the voluntary/autonomic nervous system distinction in medical texts. As we have seen above, some processes that are normally involuntary can also become partly voluntary once they are represented in consciousness (via biofeedback, imagery and so on). But if we don't have a detailed conscious awareness of the workings of our own bodies and brains and if consciousness comes too late to affect the processes to which it most closely relates how can this be? Consider again the dilemma posed by Libet *et al*'s (1979) experiments on the role of conscious volition described above. If the brain prepares to carry out a given action around 350 milliseconds before the conscious wish to act appears, then how could that action be 'conscious' and how could it be 'voluntary'? Doesn't the preceding readiness potential indicate that the action is determined preconsciously and automatically by processing in the mind/brain?

Let us consider the 'conscious' aspect first. The decision to act (indexed by the readiness potential) is taken preconsciously but it becomes conscious at the moment that it manifests *as* a wish to do something in conscious experience. The wish then becomes conscious in the same way that your perception of this WORD is conscious. Like the wish, once you become conscious of this WORD, the physical, syntactic and semantic analyses required to recognize it have already taken place. Nonetheless, once you become conscious of the wish or the WORD the mental/brain processes make a transition from a preconscious to a conscious state — and it is only when this happens that you consciously realize what is going on.[18]

But how could an act that is executed *preconsciously* be 'voluntary'? Voluntary actions imply the possibility of choice, albeit choice based on available external and internal information, current needs and goals. Voluntary actions are also potentially flexible and capable of being novel. In the psychological

---

[18] I do not have space to develop this theme in more detail here. In Velmans (2000), chs. 10, 11 and 12, I develop a broader 'reflexive monist' philosophy in which the function of consciousness is to 'real-ize' the world. That is, once an entity, event or process enters consciousness it becomes *subjectively real*.

literature these properties are traditionally associated with controlled rather than automatic processing or with focal-attentive rather than pre-attentive or non-attended processing.[19] Unlike automatic or pre-attentive processing, both controlled processing (in the execution of acts) and focal-attentive processing (in the analysis of input) are thought to be 'conscious'. None of the above argues against such traditional wisdom. In Libet's experiments the conscious experience appears around 350 milliseconds after the onset of preconscious processes that are indexed by the readiness potential. This says something about the timing of the conscious experience in relation to the processes that generate it and about its restricted role once it appears. However, it does not argue against the voluntary nature of that preconscious processing. On the contrary, the fact that the act consciously feels as if it is voluntary and controlled suggests that the processes which have generated that experience *are* voluntary and controlled, as conscious experiences generally provide reasonably accurate representations of what is going on (see above). This applies equally to the voluntary nature of more complex, mental processing such as the self-regulating, self-modifying operations of our own psychophysical minds evidenced by the effects of conscious imagery, meditation and biofeedback. In short, I suggest that the feeling that we are free to choose or to exercise control is compatible with the nature of what is actually taking place in our own central nervous system, following processes that select amongst available options, in accordance with current needs, goals, available strategies, calculations of likely consequences and so on. While I assume that such processes operate according to determinate physical principles, the system architecture that embodies them enables the ability to exercise the choice, flexibility and control that we experience — a form of biological determinism that is compatible with experienced free will.

So *who*'s in control? Who chooses, has thoughts, generates images and so on? We habitually think of ourselves as being our *conscious selves*. But it should be clear from the above that the different facets of our experienced, conscious selves are generated by and represent aspects of our own preconscious minds. That is, we are *both* the pre-conscious generating processes *and* the conscious results. Viewed from a third-person perspective our own preconscious mental processes look like neurochemical and associated physical activities in our brains. Viewed introspectively, from a first-person perspective, our preconscious mind seems like a personal but 'empty space' from which thoughts, images and feelings spontaneously arise. *We* are as much one thing as the other — and this requires a shift in our sensed 'centre of gravity' to one where our consciously experienced self becomes just the visible 'tip' of our own embedding, preconscious mind.

---

[19] Such functional differences are beyond the scope of this paper. However they have been extensively investigated, e.g. in studies of selective attention, controlled versus automatic processing, and so on (see e.g. Velmans, 1991; Kihlstrom, 1996).

APPENDIX

IS CONSCIOUSNESS NOTHING MORE
THAN A STATE OF THE BRAIN?

It has long been suspected that there is a *causal relation* between mind or consciousness and brain. For example, Hippocrates of Cos (460–357 BC) wrote that,

> Man ought to know that from the brain and from the brain only, arise our pleasures, joys, laughter and jests, as well as our sorrows, pains, griefs and fears. Through it, in particular, we think, see, hear, and distinguish the ugly from the beautiful, the bad from the good, the pleasant from the unpleasant, in some cases using custom as a test, in others perceiving them from their utility. It is the same thing which makes us mad or delirious, inspires us with dread and fear, whether by night or by day, brings sleeplessness, inopportune mistakes, aimless anxieties, absent-mindedness, and acts that are contrary to habit (from Jones, 1923; cited in Flew, 1978, p. 32).

However, the claim that mind or consciousness is *nothing more than* a state of the brain is far more radical. If this claim can be justified, then the fundamental puzzles surrounding the mind–body relationship, and (in its modern form) the consciousness–brain relationship would be solved. Clearly, if consciousness is nothing more that a state of the brain (a C-state say), it should be possible to understand it within the existing framework of natural science. Causal relations between consciousness and brain would translate into the causal relations between C-states and other brain states — and the functions of consciousness would simply be the functions of C-states within the global economy of the brain. The methods for investigating consciousness would then be third-person methods of the kind already well developed in neurophysiology and cognitive science. With such a potential prize in view, philosophical and scientific theories of consciousness over the last thirty years have in the main assumed, or tried to show, that some form of materialist reductionism is true.

How could Conscious Experiences be Brain States?

Given the apparent differences between the 'qualia' of conscious experiences and brain states it is by no means *obvious* that they are one and the same! Physicalists such as Ullin Place (1956) and J.J.C. Smart (1962) accepted that these apparent differences exist. They also accepted that descriptions of mental states and descriptions of their corresponding brain states are not identical in meaning. However, they claimed that with the advance of neurophysiology these descriptions will *be discovered* to be statements about one and the same thing. That is, a contingent rather than a logical identity will be established between consciousness, mind and brain.

Smart (1962) summarizes this position in the following way:

> Let us first try to state more accurately the thesis that sensations are brain-processes. It is not the thesis that, for example, 'after-image' or 'ache' means the same as 'brain-process of sort X' (where 'X' is replaced by a description of a certain brain process). It is that, in so far as 'after-image' or 'ache' is a report of a process, it is a report of a process that happens to be a brain process. It follows that the thesis does

not claim that sensation statements can be translated into statements about brain processes. Nor does it claim that the logic of a sensation statement is the same as that of a brain process statement. All it claims is that in so far as a sensation statement is a report of something, that something is a brain process. *Sensations are nothing over and above brain processes* (p. 163 — my italics).

In short there is a distinction to be drawn between how things seem, how we describe them, and how they really are.

It is important to remember that no discovery that reduces consciousness to brain has yet been made. Physicalism, therefore, is partly an expression of faith, based on precedents in other areas of science — and arguments in defence of this position have focused on the *kinds of discovery that would need to be made* for reductionism to be true.

C.D. Broad noted in 1925 that materialism comes in three basic versions: *radical*, *reductive* and *emergent*. Radical materialism claims that the term 'consciousness' does not refer to anything real (in contemporary philosophy this position is usually called 'eliminativism'). Reductive materialism accepts that consciousness does refer to something real, but science will discover that real thing to be nothing more than a state (or function) of the brain. Emergentism also accepts the reality of consciousness but claims it to be a higher-order property of brains; it supervenes on neural activity, but cannot be reduced to it.

While it is not the purpose of this Appendix to give a full appraisal of these positions (I do this elsewhere — Velmans, 2000, chs. 3, 4 and 5) it may be useful to indicate why I do not adopt them. So, by way of illustration, I list some of problems that physicalism must solve, some of the more plausible physicalist solutions to these, and a few of the problems with the solutions below.

What Non-Eliminative Reductionism Needs to Show

Let us assume that, in some sense, our conscious experiences are real. To each and every one of us, our conscious experiences are observable *phenomena* (psychological *data*) which we can describe with varying degrees of accuracy in ordinary language. *Other* people's experiences might be hypothetical constructs, as we cannot observe their experiences in the direct way that we can observe our own, but that does not make our own experiences similarly hypothetical. Nor are our own conscious experiences 'theories' or 'folk psychologies'. We may have everyday theories *about* what we experience, and with deeper insight we might be able to improve them, but this would not replace or necessarily improve the experiences themselves.

In essence then, the claim that conscious experiences are nothing more than brain states is a claim about one set of phenomena (first-person experiences of love, hate, the smell of mown grass, the colour of a sunset, etc.) being nothing more than another set of phenomena (brain states, viewed from the perspective of an external observer). Given the extensive, apparent differences between conscious experiences and brain states this is a tall order. Formally, one must establish that despite appearances, conscious experiences are *ontologically identical* to brain states.

Instances where phenomena viewed from one perspective turned out to be one and the same as seemingly different phenomena viewed from another perspective do occur in the history of science. A classical example is the way the 'morning star' and the 'evening star' turned out to be identical (they were both found to be the planet Venus). But viewing consciousness from a first- versus a third-person perspective is very different to seeing the same planet in the morning or the evening. From a third-person (external observer's) perspective one has *no direct access* to a subject's conscious experience. Consequently, one has no third-person data (about the experience itself) which can be compared to or contrasted with the subject's first-person data. Neurophysiological investigations are limited, in principle, to isolating the neural correlates or antecedent causes of given experiences. This would be a major scientific advance. But what would it tell us about the nature of consciousness itself?

Common Reductionist Arguments and Fallacies

Reductionists commonly argue that if one can find the neural *causes* or *correlates* of consciousness in the brain, then this would establish consciousness *itself* to be a brain state (see for example, Place, 1956; Crick, 1994). Let us call these the 'causation argument' and the 'correlation argument'. I suggest that such arguments are based on a fairly obvious fallacy. For consciousness to be nothing more than a brain state, it must be *ontologically identical* to a brain state. However, *correlation* and *causation* do not establish *ontological identity*. These relationships have been persistently confounded in the literature. So let me make the differences clear.

Ontological identity is *symmetrical*; that is, if A is identical to B, then B is identical to A. Ontological identity also *obeys Leibniz's Law*: if A is identical to B, all the properties of A are also properties of B, and vice-versa (for example all the properties of the 'morning star' are also properties of the 'evening star').

Correlation is also *symmetrical*; if A correlates with B, then B correlates with A. But correlation does *not obey Leibniz's Law*; if A correlates with B, it does not follow that all the properties of A and B are the same. For example, height in humans correlates with weight, but height and weight do not have the same set of properties.

Causation, by contrast, is *asymmetrical*; if A causes B, it does not follow that B causes A. If a rock thrown in a pond causes ripples in the water, it does not follow that ripples in the water cause the rock to be thrown in the pond. And causation does *not obey Leibniz's Law* (flying rocks and pond ripples have very different properties).

Once the obvious differences between causation, correlation and ontological identity are laid bare the weaknesses of the 'causation argument' and the 'correlation argument' are clear. Under appropriate conditions, brain states may be shown to cause, or correlate with conscious experiences, but it does not follow that conscious experiences are nothing more than states (or, for that matter, functions) of the brain. To demonstrate that, one would have to establish an ontological identity in which all the properties of a conscious experience and corresponding brain state are identical. Unfortunately for reductionism, few if any properties of experiences (accurately described) and brain states appear to be identical.

In short, the causes and correlates of conscious experience should not be confused with their *ontology*. As it happens, various *nonreductionist* positions such as dualist-interactionism, epiphenomenalism and modern dual-aspect theory *agree* that consciousness (in humans) is causally influenced by and correlates with neural events, but they *deny* that consciousness is nothing more than a state of the brain. As no information about consciousness *other than its neural causes and correlates* is available to neurophysiological investigation of the brain, it is difficult to see how such research could ever settle the issue. The *only* evidence about what conscious experiences are like comes from first-person sources, which consistently suggest consciousness to be something other than or additional to neuronal activity. Given this, I conclude that reductionism via this route *cannot be made to work* (cf. Velmans, 1998).

False Analogies

Faced with this difficulty, reductionists usually turn to analogies from other areas in science, where a reductive, causal account of a phenomenon led to an understanding of its ontology, very different to its phenomenology. Francis Crick (1994), for example, makes the point that in science, reductionism is both common and successful. Genes for example turned out to be nothing but DNA molecules. So, in science, this is the best way to proceed. While he recognizes that experienced (first-person) 'qualia' pose a problem for reductionism, he suggests that in the fullness of time it may be possible to describe the *neural correlates* of such qualia. If we can understand the nature of the correlates we may come to understand the corresponding forms of consciousness. By these means science will show that 'You're nothing but a pack of neurones!'.

It should be apparent from the above that finding the neural correlates of consciousness won't be enough to reduce people to neurones! The reduction of consciousness to brain is also quite unlike the reduction of genes to DNA. In the development of genetics, 'genes' were initially hypothetical entities inferred to exist to account for observed regularities in the transmission of characteristics from parents to offspring. The discovery that genes are DNA molecules shows how a theoretical entity is sometimes discovered to be 'real'. A similar discovery was made for bacteria, which were inferred causes of disease until the development of the microscope, after which they could be seen. Viruses remained hypothetical until the development of the electron microscope, after which they too could be seen. These are genuine cases of materialist reduction (of hypothetical to physical entities).

But it would be absurd to regard conscious experiences as 'hypothetical entities', waiting for their neural substrates to be discovered to make them real. Conscious experiences are first-person *phenomena*. To those who have them, they provide the very fabric of subjective reality. One does not have to wait for the advance of neuroscience to know that one has been stung by a bee! If conscious experiences *were* merely hypothetical, the mind–body problems, and in particular the problems posed by the phenomenal properties of 'qualia' would not exist.

Ullin Place (1956) focuses on causation rather than correlation. As he notes, we now understand lightning to be nothing more than the motion of electrical charges through the atmosphere. But mere correlations of lightning with electrical discharges do not suffice to justify this reduction. Rather, he argues, the reduction is justified once we know that the motion of electrical charges through the atmosphere *causes* what we experience as lightning. Similarly, a conscious experience may be said to be a given state of the brain once we know that brain state to have *caused* the conscious experience.

I have dealt with the fallacy of the 'causation argument' above. But the lightning analogy is seductive because it is half-true. That is, *for the purposes of physics* it is true that lightning can be described as nothing more than the motion of electrical charges. But there are three things that need to be accounted for in this situation, not just one — an event in the world, a perceiver, and a resulting experience. Physics is interested in the nature of the event in the world. However, psychology is interested in how this physical event interacts with a visual system to produce *experienced lightning* — in the form of a perceived flash of light in a phenomenal world. This experienced lightning may be said to *represent* the same event in the world which physics describes as a motion of electrical charges. But the *phenomenology of the experience itself* cannot be said to be nothing more than the motion of electrical charges! Prior to the emergence of life forms with visual systems on this planet, there presumably was no such phenomenology, although the electrical charges which now give rise to this experience did exist.

In sum, the fact that motions of electrical charges cause the experience of lightning does not warrant the conclusion that the *phenomenology* of the experience is nothing more than the motion of electrical charges. Nor would finding the neurophysiological causes of conscious experiences warrant the reduction of the phenomenology of those experiences to states of the brain.

Given that examples of first-person reduction to third-person science (DNA, lightning, colour, heat, etc.) are not really examples of first-person reduction at all, perhaps a nonreductive materialism is more appropriate. For example, according to Searle (1987; 1992; 1994a; 1997) conscious states cannot be redescribed (now or ever) in neurophysiological language. Rather, they have to be described just as they seem to be. Searle, for example, believes *subjectivity* and *intentionality* to be essential features of consciousness. Conscious states have 'intrinsic intentionality', that is, it is intrinsic to them that they are *about* something. According to Searle, this distinguishes conscious states from physical representations such as sentences written on a page. Conscious readers might interpret these *as if* they are about something (such physical representations have 'as-if intentionality'), but they are just marks on a piece of paper and not about anything in themselves. Subjectivity, too, 'is unlike anything else in biology, and in a sense it is one of the most amazing features of nature' (Searle 1994a, p. 97). Nevertheless, he maintains that conscious states are just higher-order features of the brain.

Emergentism

In classical dualism, consciousness is thought to be a nonmaterial substance or entity different in kind from the material world, with an existence that is independent of the existence of the brain (although in normal life it interacts with the brain). 'Emergentism' in the form of 'property dualism' retains the view that there are fundamental differences between consciousness and physical matter, but views these as different kinds of property of the brain. That is, consciousness is not *reducible* but its existence is still *dependent* on the workings of the brain — and according to Searle, such a non-reducible brain property is still 'physical'.

Searle (1987), for example, argues that *causality* should not be confused with *ontological identity* (as I do in my critique of reductionism above), and his case for physicalism appears to be one of the few to have addressed this distinction head-on. The gap between what *causes* consciousness and what conscious *is* can be bridged, he suggests, by an understanding of how microproperties relate to macroproperties. Liquidity of water is caused by the way H_2O molecules slide over each other, but is nothing more than (an emergent property of) the combined effect of these molecular movements. Likewise, solidity is caused by the way molecules in crystal lattices bind to each other, but is nothing more than the higher order (emergent) effect of such bindings. In similar fashion, consciousness is caused by neuronal activity in the brain and is nothing more than the higher order, emergent effect of such activity. That is, consciousness is just a *physical macroproperty* of the brain.

Searle's argument is attractive, but it needs to be examined with care. The brain undoubtedly has physical macroproperties of many kinds. Like other physical systems, its physical microstructure supports a physical macrostructure. However, the physical macroproperty of brains that is most closely analogous to 'solidity' and 'liquidity' is 'sponginess', not consciousness! There are, of course, more psychologically relevant macroproperties, for example the blood flow patterns picked up by PET scans or the magnetic and electrical activities detected by fMRI and EEG. But why should increased blood flow constitute subjectivity, or why would it be 'like anything' to be an electrical potential or magnetic field? While some of these properties undoubtedly *correlate* with conscious experiences, there is little reason to suppose that they are *ontologically identical* to conscious experiences.

One might also question how Searle's property dualism could really be a form of *physicalism*. Searle insists that consciousness is a *physical* phenomenon, produced by the brain in the sense that the gall bladder produces bile. But he also stresses that *subjectivity* and *intentionality* are defining characteristics of consciousness. Unlike physical phenomena, the phenomenology of consciousness cannot be observed from the outside; unlike physical phenomena, it is always *of* or *about* something. So, even one accepts that consciousness is, in some sense, caused by or emergent from the brain, why call it 'physical' as opposed to 'mental' or 'psychological'? Merely *relabelling* consciousness, or moving from micro- to macroproperties doesn't really close the gap between 'objective' brains and 'subjective' experiences![20]

In sum, demonstrating the brain to have physical macroproperties that are supervenient on its physical microproperties is one thing; *identifying* those physical macroproperties with the properties of *consciousness* is another! Searle, as shown above, tries to settle the issue by *fiat*. Subjective, intentional conscious experiences are simply *declared* to be physical states. But this doesn't really help much. The ontology of these 'new' physical states is not really clarified by renaming them. Nor does the transition from smaller things to larger things (from microproperties to macroproperties) really *explain* how material brains viewed from a third-person perspective could themselves have a conscious, first-person perspective! Further, the problem of *how* such extraordinary 'subjective', 'intentional' states could *interact* with ordinary physical states remains. (A fuller analysis of Searle's position, taking account of his 1997 defence, is given in Velmans, 2000, ch. 3.)

---

[20] I should stress that I do not deny that conscious experiences can be said to 'emerge' from the human brain in the sense that given brain states can be said to *cause* given conscious experiences. That is, I do not deny the legitimacy of physical→mental causal accounts, anymore than I deny the legitimacy of physical→pysical, mental→pysical and mental→mental accounts. The question is: how do we make sense of these accounts? The physicalist answer (in whatever guise it takes) is to translate all these causal accounts into physical→physical accounts — in this case, by trying to show that conscious states are nothing more than higher-order, emergent *physical* states of the brain. As far as I can tell, this manoeuvre cannot really be made to work. That is, first-person consciousness cannot be thought of as a 'physical' property of the brain in any conventional, third-person sense of the term 'physical'. Note that the problems of *identifying* first-person consciousness with third-person features persist even when we select plausible, emergent brain properties that are less obviously 'physical', but nevertheless describable in third-person, functional terms. For example, Dewar (1976) (elaborating on the emergent-interactionism of Roger Sperry, 1969) cites the phenomenon of 'mutual entrainment'. The term 'entrainment' refers to the synchronization of an oscillator to an input signal. This occurs, for example, when television receiver oscillators controlling the vertical and horizontal lines 'lock into' transmitting frequencies to produce a given picture on the screen. Examples of entrainment, Dewar notes, may also be found at many levels of biological organization — a particularly apposite case being the way 'biological clocks' governing circadian rhythms can be locked into varying periods (of around 24 hours) to produce altered cycles of day–night activity in animals. 'Mutual entrainment' occurs when two or more oscillators interact in such a way that they pull one another into synchrony. This occurs, for example, when different alternating-current generators feeding the national grid are pulled into synchrony by what Norbert Wiener refers to as a 'virtual governor' in the system. Although the generators may be far distant from each other and may start up and stop at idiosyncratic times, once 'on-line' they are made to speed up or slow down to produce AC current in phase with that of all the other machines feeding the grid. As Dewar points out the 'virtual governor' is not located in any one place in the system, but rather pervades the system as a whole so that it does not have a 'physical existence' in the usual sense. It is an emergent property of the entire system. In similar fashion, Dewar suggests, consciousness is 'a holistic emergent property of the interaction of neurones which has the power to be self-reflective and ascertain its own awareness'.

This analogy becomes particularly interesting in the light of the suggestion that synchronous or correlated firing of diverse neurone groups (at rhythmic frequencies in the 40 Hz region) might produce the 'neural binding' required to produce an integrated experience from features of objects that are encoded in spatially separated regions of the brain. Given the well-integrated nature of normal conscious experiences, it seems reasonable to propose that binding processes operate prior to the formation of, or co-occur with, such experiences. However, there is little reason to suggest that 'binding' or 'mutual entrainment' is *ontologically identical* to consciousness — unless we are willing to accept that the national grid is conscious. How mutual entrainment or binding 'has the power to be self-reflective and ascertain its own awareness' remains a mystery! (A more detailed analysis of how consciousness relates to mutual entrainment and binding is given in Velmans, 2000, pp. 41–2).

References

Baars, B.J. and McGovern, K. (1996), 'Cognitive views of consciousness: What are the facts? How can we explain them?', in Velmans (1996a).

Barber, T.X. (1984), 'Changing "unchangeable" bodily processes by (hypnotic) suggestions: a new look at hypnosis, cognitions, imagining, and the mind body problem', in *Imagination and Healing*, ed. A.A. Sheikh (Farmingdale, NY: Bayworld).

Boomer, D.S. (1970), 'Review of F. Goldman-Eisler *Psycholinguistics: Experiments in Spontaneous Speech'*, *Lingua*, **25**, pp. 152–64.

Broad, C.D. (1925), *The Mind and Its Place in Nature* (London: Routledge & Kegan Paul).

Chalmers, D.J. (1996), *The Conscious Mind* (New York: Oxford University Press).

Crick, F. (1994), *The Astonishing Hypothesis* (London: Simon & Schuster).

Dewar, E.M. (1976), 'Consciousness in control systems theory', in *Consciousness and the Brain*, ed. G.G. Globus, G. Maxwell and I. Savodnik (New York: Plenum).

Flew, A. (ed. 1978), *Body, Mind, and Death* (New York: Macmillan Publishing).

Fodor, J.A., Bever, T.G. and Garrett, M.F. (1974), *The Psychology of Language* (New York: McGraw-Hill).

Gardner, H. (1987), *The Mind's New Science* (New York: Basic Books).

Goldman-Eisler, F. (1968), *Psycholinguistics* (New York: Academic Press).

Hashish, I., Finman, C. and Harvey, W. (1988), 'Reduction of postoperative pain and swelling by ultrasound: a placebo effect', *Pain*, **83**, pp. 303–11.

Kanttinen, N. and Lyytinen, H. (1993), 'Brain slow waves preceding time-locked visuo-motor performance', *Journal of Sport Sciences*, **11**, pp. 257–66.

Karrer, R., Warren, C. and Ruth, R. (1978), 'Slow potentials of the brain preceding cued and non-cued movement: effects of development and retardation', in *Multidisciplinary Perspectives in Event-Related Potential Research*, ed. D.A. Otto (Washington DC: US Government Printing Office).

Kihlstrom, J.F. (1996), 'Perception without awareness of what is perceived, learning without awareness of what is learned', in Velmans (1996a).

Kornhuber, H.H. and Deecke, L. (1965), 'Hirnpotentialänderungen bei willkürbewegungen und passiven bewegungen des menchen: Bereitschaftspotential und reafferente potentiale', *Pflügers Archiv für die Gesampte Physiologie des Menschen und Tiere*, **284**, pp. 1–17.

Lenneberg, E.H. (1967), *Biological Foundations of Language* (New York: Wiley).

Libet, B. (1985), 'Unconscious cerebral initiative and the role of conscious will in voluntary action', *Behavioral and Brain Sciences*, **8**, pp. 529–66.

Libet, B. (1996), 'Neural processes in the production of conscious experience', in Velmans (1996a).

Libet, B., Wright Jr., E.W., Feinstein, B. and Pearl, D.K. (1979), 'Subjective referral of the timing for a conscious experience: A functional role for the somatosensory specific projection system in man', *Brain*, **102**, pp. 193–224.

Mangan, B. (1993), 'Taking phenomenology seriously: The 'fringe' and its implications for cognitive research', *Consciousness and Cognition*, **2** (2), pp. 89–108.

McMahon, C.E. and Sheikh, A. (1989), 'Psychosomatic illness: a new look', in *Eastern and Western Approaches to Healing*, ed. A. Sheikh and K. Sheikh (New York: Wiley-Interscience).

Pelletier, K.R. (1993), 'Between mind and body: stress, emotions, and health', in *Mind Body Medicine*, ed. D. Goleman and J. Gurin (New York: Consumer Reports Books).

Place, U. (1956), 'Is consciousness a brain process?', *British Journal of Psychology*, **47**, pp. 44–50.

Rakover, S.S. (1996), 'The place of consciousness in the information processing approach: The mental pool thought experiment', *Behavioral and Brain Sciences*, **19** (3), pp. 535–6.

Searle, J. (1987), 'Minds and brains without programs', in *Mindwaves*, ed. C. Blakemore and S. Greenfield (Oxford: Blackwell).

Searle, J. (1992), *The Rediscovery of the Mind* (Cambridge, MA: MIT Press).

Searle, J. (1994a), 'The problem of consciousness', in *Consciousness in Philosophy and Cognitive Neuroscience*, ed. A. Revonsuo and M. Kamppinen (Hillsdale, NJ: Lawrence Erlbaum Assoc.).

Searle, J. (1994b), 'Intentionality (1)', in *A Companion to the Philosophy of Mind*, ed. S. Guttenplan (Oxford: Blackwell).

Searle, J. (1997), *The Mystery of Consciousness* (London: Granta Books).

Smart, J.J.C. (1962), 'Sensations and brain processes', in *Philosophy of Mind*, ed. V.C. Chappell (Englewood Cliffs: Prentice-Hall).

Sheikh, A.A. (ed. 2001), *Healing Images: The Role of Imagination in the Healing Process* (Amityville, NY: Baywood Publishing Company).

Sheikh, A.A., Kunzendorf, R.G. and Sheikh, K.S. (1996), 'Somatic consequences of consciousness', in Velmans (1996a).

Skrabanek, P. & McCormick, J. (1989), *Follies and Fallacies in Medicine* (Glasgow: The Tarragon Press).

Sperry, R.W. (1969), 'A modified concept of consciousness', *Psychological Review*, **76** (6), pp. 532–6.

Stoffregen, T.A. and Benoît, G.B. (2001), 'On specification of the senses', *Behavioral and Brain Sciences*, **24** (2), pp. 195–261.

Syrjala, K.A. and Abrams, J.R. (1996), 'Hypnosis and imagery in the treatment of pain', in *Psychological Approaches to Pain Management: A Practitioner's Handbook*, ed. R.J. Catchel and D.C. Turk (New York: The Guildford Press).

Tye, M. (1995), *Ten Problems of Consciousness: A Representational Theory of the Phenomenal Mind* (Cambridge, MA: MIT Press).

Velmans, M. (1990), 'Consciousness, brain, and the physical world', *Philosophical Psychology*, **3**, pp. 77–99.

Velmans, M. (1991a), 'Is human information processing conscious?', *Behavioral and Brain Sciences*, **14** (4), pp. 651–69.

Velmans, M. (1991b), 'Consciousness from a first-person perspective', *Behavioral and Brain Sciences*, **14** (4), pp. 702–26.

Velmans, M. (1993), 'Consciousness, causality and complementarity', *Behavioral and Brain Sciences*, **16** (2), pp. 409–16.

Velmans, M. (ed. 1996a), *The Science of Consciousness: Psychological, Neuropsychological and Clinical Reviews* (London: Routledge).

Velmans, M. (1996b), 'Consciousness and the "causal paradox"', *Behavioral and Brain Sciences*, **19** (3), pp. 538–42.

Velmans, M. (1998), 'Goodbye to reductionism', in *Towards a Science of Consciousness II: The Second Tucson Discussions and Debates*, ed. S. Hameroff, A. Kaszniak and A. Scott (Cambridge, MA: MIT Press).

Velmans, M. (2000), *Understanding Consciousness* (London: Routledge/Psychology Press).

Velmans, M. (2001a), 'A natural account of phenomenal consciousness', *Consciousness and Communication*, **34** (1&2), pp. 39–59.

Velmans, M. (2001b), 'Heterophenomenology versus critical phenomenology: A dialogue with Dan Dennett', http://cogprints.soton.ac.uk/documents/disk0/00/00/17/95/index.html

Wall, P.D. (1996), 'The placebo effect', in *The Science of Consciousness: Psychological, Neuropsychological and Clinical Reviews*, ed. M. Velmans (London: Routledge).

Watkins, A. (1997), 'Mind–body pathways', in *Mind–Body Medicine: A Clinician's Guide to Psychoneuroimmunology*, ed. A. Watkins (New York: Churchill Livingstone).

Watt, D. (2000), 'The centrencephalon and thalamocortical integration: Neglected contributions of periaqueductal gray', *Consciousness and Emotion*, **1** (1), pp. 91–11.

Peer Commentary

THE SEDUCTIONS OF MATERIALISM
AND THE PLEASURES OF DUALISM

John F. Kihlstrom

We're all materialists now. Among those who retain the Cartesian categories of mind and body, even the Mysterians agree that the mind is what the brain does, even if they despair of knowing how it does it (McGinn, 1991; 1999). And for those biological naturalists who reject the Cartesian categories (Searle, 1992; 1999), consciousness is a feature of brains that have achieved a certain level of organization. The materialist consensus links psychology, William James' (James, 1890/1980) science of mental life, with the other natural sciences, such as biology, chemistry, and physics, and for that reason it has been very seductive. However, as Velmans cogently points out in his target article, it does not offer a complete solution to the problem of consciousness, not least because it promotes premature closure on some problems and leaves others unaddressed. Among these unaddressed questions is whether, to what extent, and how conscious mental states — or *unconscious* ones, for that matter (Kihlstrom, 1987) — can have a causal influence on bodily functions. If we are to take consciousness seriously, as more than epiphenomenal, then we need to show that it has causal powers: that what we think, feel, or want actually has an effect on what we do.

In all of this debate, one relevant body of evidence tends to be ignored: the so-called 'psychosomatic' disorders known to psychiatry, in which a mental state, usually emotional in nature, appears to cause some bodily symptom, such as an ulcer (Graham, 1972; Weiner, 1977). In large part, I suspect that this neglect occurred because the psychosomatic disorders have long been tainted by some of the very worst sort of psychoanalytic thinking. For example, Franz Alexander (1950) argued that a whole host of physical diseases could have their origins in unconscious and unresolved 'nuclear conflicts': anorexia nervosa was caused by envy and jealousy, peptic ulcers were caused by conflicts between infantile dependency versus ego pride and aspiration, bronchial asthma was caused by excessive unresolved dependence on one's mother, essential hypertension was caused by chronically inhibited aggressive impulses, rheumatoid arthritis was caused by rebellion against restrictive parental influences, and so on.

It would be generous to say that the evidence for propositions such as these is weak, based as it is on subjective impressions of personality in individual cases of unknown representativeness without adequate controls. Moreover, to some extent discussion of psychological causes of physical illnesses has been impeded by advances in biomedical knowledge about both 'physical' and 'mental' disease processes. So, for example, it is common to see such psychiatric syndromes as depression, anxiety, and schizophrenia identified as 'real diseases' because we now think we know something about their neurobiological underpinnings in the amygdala, dopamine, the human genome, or whatever — as if these mental illnesses were not real until they had been characterized in neurobiological terms. As another example, the discovery of the role of *Helicobacter pylori* in gastric ulcers (Marshall & Warren, 1984) led Steven E. Hyman, later to become the Director of the National Institute of Mental Health, to gleefully report that 'Another One Bites the Dust' (Hyman, 1994), and to question 'the allure of attributing... illnesses primarily to psychological factors' (p. 295). Unfortunately for the argument, it turns out that while a large proportion of ulcer patients may be infected with *H. pylori*, a high rate of infection is also found in people *without* ulcers (Nomura *et al.*, 1994). In other words, bacterial infection may be *necessary* for ulcers to occur, but it is not *sufficient* for them to occur, as even the discoverer of *H. pylori* himself seems to agree (Marshall, 1995).

In fact, animal research shows a clear role for stress in the predisposing organisms to ulcers, precipitating ulcers, and sustaining ulcers once they have developed (Overmier & Murison, 1997; 2000; Weiss, 1972). Although 'stress' is in some sense a physiological construct, in terms of any event that challenges an organism's current level of adaptation (Selye, 1956), in this research 'stress' refers specifically to a mental state. Beginning in the 1960s, the cognitive revolution in learning theory led to a reinterpretation of classical conditioning in terms of the organism's efforts to predict environmental events (Kamin, 1969; Rescorla, 1967), and of instrumental conditioning in terms of the organism's efforts to gain control over environmental events (Maier & Seligman, 1976; Seligman & Maier, 1967). In psychology, organisms (including people) are stressed when they are exposed to unpredictable and unavoidable events, especially if these are aversive (Mineka & Kihlstrom, 1978; Seligman *et al.*, 1971). To the extent that psychological stress is a *psychological*, i.e., *mental*, state, then, the literature on ulcers yields clear evidence of an effect of the mind on the body. We now know that stress, defined psychologically as the exposure to unpredictable and/or unavoidable aversive events, is sufficient to produce ulcers.

Another area of relevant research is on Viagra (sildenafil ciltrate), the well-known (and increasingly popular) treatment for male erectile dysfunction marketed by Pfizer. Viagra is a pill, and so we might assume that its mechanism of action is purely physiological. And for the most part, it is: according to Pfizer's package insert, sildenafil selectively inhibits phosphodiesterase type 5 (PDE5), which in turn enhances the effect of nitric oxide (NO) on the release of cyclic guanosine monophosphate (cGMP), causing muscle relaxation and vasodilation in the corpus cavernosum, and the increased bloodflow results in tumescence and full erection. It's all a matter of biochemistry, except — as Pfizer's package inserts and advertising clearly state, none of this occurs in the absence of sexual stimulation, which is what releases NO in the first place. This sexual stimulation may be tactile (Maytom *et al.*, 1999), in which case we may be dealing with a simple spinal reflex, or it may be visual (Boolell *et al.*, 1996), in which case we are dealing with something much less reflexive, and something much closer to an intentional mental state. Unfortunately, there have been no published studies of the effects of Viagra in the absence of any kind of sexual stimulation. But the available literature suggests that, in the absence of tactile stimulation, the biochemical mechanics of Viagra begin with a conscious mental state of sexual arousal.

The experiences of unpredictability and uncontrollability are mental states in the strict sense: they are *beliefs* that the world, or some important aspect of it, is unpredictable, uncontrollable, or both. And sexual arousal is also a mental state, a state of sexual desire. Accordingly, they possess intentionality, or 'aboutness' (Searle, 1983; 1992). But they are not particularly specific beliefs like *John believes it is raining* or *John wants a pizza*. Is there evidence for the psychosomatic role of more specific beliefs about more specific things? One relevant body of research concerns the placebo effect in medicine, where a therapeutic change occurs by virtue of the patient's belief that he or she is receiving an effective treatment — and, perhaps, his or her doctor's belief that he or she is administering one (Harrington, 1997; Shapiro & Shapiro, 1997). Placebo effects have been called the 'jewel in the crown' of 'mind–body' medicine, and as such make biologically oriented physicians very nervous — which may be one reason that there are occasional attempts to demonstrate that they don't exist (Hrobjartsson & Gotzsche, 2001), or to argue that they only affect subjective, mental symptoms such as depression and pain, in which case they don't really count as examples of psychosomatic interaction (Spiro, 1986). But there is some reason to believe that placebos can have genuine effects on objectively observed bodily functioning, as measured by dopamine release in Parkinson's disease (de la Fuente *et al.*, 2001), improved knee function in osteoarthritis (Bradley *et al.*, 2002), and changes in brain function in depressed patients (Leuchter *et al.*, 2002). In these cases, at least, we have more than an effect of one belief — that one has received an effective treatment — on another belief — that one is depressed or in pain. We have a genuine effect of a belief on the body.

Placebo effects are usually defined as nonspecific in nature, but some research indicates that they can be very specific indeed. In the domain of pain, for example, two placebos yield more relief than one, and placebo injections more than placebo pills (Evans, 1974). More recently, it has been shown that placebos administered to relieve pain in one part of the body have no effect on pain in another part of the body. Perhaps most dramatically, an analysis by Evans revealed that placebo efficiency was a constant function of the active drug to which placebo was compared (Evans, 1974): placebo aspirin is 54% as effective as aspirin, placebo Darvon is 56% as effective as Darvon, and placebo morphine is 56% as effective as morphine. Evans' findings have been questioned in some quarters (McQuay *et al.*, 1995), but the later studies varied significantly in design from the ones Evans reviewed. Although it remains to be seen whether Evans' findings generalize to objective as well as subjective endpoints, it appears that the effectiveness of a placebo depends on what drug the patients *believe* they are taking.

Turning to the effects of belief on objectively measurable physical outcomes, there are a number of studies showing the psychosomatic effects of both hypnotic and nonhypnotic suggestion (Bowers, 1977; Bowers & Kelly, 1979). In one classic study, 11 of 13 patients who were sensitive to a form of contact dermatitis similar to poison ivy showed a diminished skin reaction when exposed to the plant when they believed the leaf was harmless, and 12 of 13 showed signs of dermatitis when exposed to a harmless plant, which they believed was poisonous (Ikemi and Nakagawa, 1962). Similar results were obtained in more recent symptom-provocation studies of asthma (Luparcllo *et al.*, 1968) and of food allergies (Jewett *et al.*, 1990). Another series of carefully designed studies showed that subjects who received verbal suggestions showed increased regression of warts, compared to those who received either a placebo or no treatment (Spanos *et al.*, 1988; 1990). In one particularly provocative study, asthmatic patients were administered either a bronchoconstrictor or a bronchodilator. Patients who received the bronchoconstrictor correctly identified as such showed greater airway response than those to whom the drug was identified as a dilator; and similarly, those who received the bronchodilator correctly identified as such showed increased greater response than those for whom it was identified as a constrictor (Luparello *et al.*, 1970).

More research on psychosomatic interactions is clearly in order, once the medical community starts taking them seriously again. Still, the evidence available so far clearly indicates that people's conscious beliefs can play a powerful role in creating and modifying their bodily states. Consciousness is not just an effect of bodily activity, and it is not merely epiphenomenal froth on the wave of neural connections. Consciousness also has causal efficacy, by virtue of its effects on bodily states, and one of the pleasures of dualism is that it reminds us that mind matters. Velmans is right to draw attention to this literature, and to take it seriously. I think he is also right that we will never solve the mind–body problem so long as we focus our attention on the mysterious leap between body and mind, and ignore the equally mysterious link between mind and body.

Author Note

Preparation of this paper supported by Grant #MH-35856 from the National Institute of Mental Health. A longer version, with some comments on reductionism, is available at: http://socrates.berkeley.edu/~kihlstrm/Velmans02_long.htm.

References

Alexander, F. (1950), *Psychosomatic Medicine: Its principles and applications* (New York: Norton).

Boolell, M., Gepi-Attee, S., Gingell, J.C. & Allen, M.J. (1996), 'Sildenafil, a novel effective oral therapy for male erectile dysfunction', *British Journal of Urology*, **78**, pp. 257–61.

Bowers, K.S. (1977), 'Hypnosis: An informational approach', *Annals of the New York Academy of Sciences*, **296**, pp. 222–37.

Bowers, K.S., & Kelly, P. (1979), 'Stress, disease, psychotherapy, and hypnosis', *Journal of Abnormal Psychology*, **88**, pp. 506–26.

Bradley, J.D., Heilman, D.K., Katz, B.P., Gsell, P., Wallick, J.E. & Brandt, K.D. (2002), 'Tidal irrigation as treatment for knee osteoarthritis: A sham-controlled, randomized, double-blinded evaluation', *Arthritis & Rheumatism*, **46**, pp. 100–8.

de la Fuente, R., Ruth, T.J., Sossi, V., Schulzer, M., Caine, D.B. & Stoessl, A. J. (2001), 'Expectation and dopamine release: Mechanism of the placebo effect in Parkinson's disease', *Science*, **293**, pp. 1164–6.

Evans, F.J. (1974), 'The placebo response in pain reduction', in *Advances in Neurology*, ed. J.J. Bonica (New York: Raven).

Graham, D.T. (1972), 'Psychosomatic medicine', in *Handbook of Psychophysiology*, ed. N.S. Greenfield & R.A. Sternbach (New York: Holt, Rinehart & Winston).
Harrington, A. (ed. 1997), *The Placebo Effect* (Cambridge, MA: Harvard University Press).
Hrobjartsson, A. & Gotzsche, P.C. (2001), 'Is the placebo powerless? An analysis of clinical trials comparing placebo with no treatment', *New England Journal of Medicine*, **344** (21), pp. 1594–602.
Hyman, S.E. (1994), 'Another one bites the dust: An infectious origin for peptic ulcers', *Harvard Review of Psychiatry*, **1**, pp. 294–5.
Ikemi, Y. & Nakagawa, S. (1962), 'A psychosomatic study of contagious dermatitis', *Kyushu Journal of Medical Science*, **13**.
James, W. (1890/1980), *Principles of Psychology* (Cambridge, MA: Harvard University Press).
Jewett, D.L., Fein, G. & Greenberg, M.H. (1990), 'A double-blind study of symptom provocation to determine food sensitivity', *New England Journal of Medicine*, **323**, pp. 429–33.
Kamin, L.J. (1969), 'Predictability, surprise, attention, and conditioning', in *Punishment and Aversive Behavior*, ed. B.A. Campbell & R.M. Church (New York: Appleton-Century Crofts).
Kihlstrom, J.F. (1987), 'The cognitive unconscious', *Science*, **237** (4821), pp. 1445–52.
Leuchter, A.F., Cook, I.A., Witte, E.A., Morgan, M.M. & Abrams, M. (2002), 'Changes in brain function of depressed subjects during treatment with placebo', *American Journal of Psychiatry*, **159**, pp. 122–9.
Luparello, T.J., Leist, N. & Lourie, C.H. (1970), 'The interaction of psychologic stimuli and pharmacologic agents on airway reactivity in asthmatic subjects', *Psychosomatic Medicine*, **32**, pp. 509–13.
Luparello, T.J., Lyons, H., Bleecker, E.R. & McFadden, E.R. (1968), 'Influences of suggestion on airway reactivity in asthmatic subjects', *Psychosomatic Medicine*, **30**, pp. 819–25.
Maier, S.F. & Seligman, M.E.P. (1976), 'Learned helplessness: Theory and evidence', *Journal of Experimental Psychology: General*, **81**, pp. 94–100.
Marshall, B.J. (1995), '*Helicobacter pulori* in peptic ulcer: Have Koch's postulates been fulfilled?', *Annals of Medicine*, **27**, pp. 565–8.
Marshall, B.J. & Warren, J.R. (1984), 'Unidentified curved bacilli in the stomach of patients with gastritis and peptic ulceration', *Lancet*, **1**, p. 1311.
Maytom, M.C., Derry, F.A., Dinsmore, W.W., Glass, C.A., Smith, M.D., Orr, M. & Ostrloh, I.H. (1999), 'A two-part pilut study of sildenafil (VIAGRA) in men with erectile dysfunction caused by spinal cord injury', *Spinal Cord*, **37**, pp. 110–16.
McGinn, C. (1991), *The Problem of Consciousness : Essays towards a resolution* (Oxford: Blackwell).
McGinn, C. (1999), *The Mysterious Flame: Conscious minds in a material world* (New York: Basic Books).
McQuay, H., Carroll, D. & Moore, A. (1995), 'Variation in the placebo effect in randomised controlled trials of analgesics: All is as blind as it seems', *Pain*, **64**, pp. 331–5.
Mineka, S. & Kihlstrom, J.F. (1978), 'Unpredictable and uncontrollable events: A new perspective on experimental neurosis', *Journal of Abnormal Psychology*, **87** (2), pp. 256–71.
Nomura, A., Stemmermann, G.N., Chyou, P-H., Perez-Perez, G.I. & Blaser, M.J. (1994), '*Helicobacter pylori* infection and the risk for duodenal and gastric ulceration', *Annals of Internal Medicine*, **120**, pp. 977–81.
Overmier, J.B., & Murison, R. (1997), 'Animal models reveal the "psych" in the psychosomatics of ulcers', *Current Directions in Psychological Science*, **6** (6), pp. 180–4.
Overmier, J.B., & Murison, R. (2000), 'Anxiety and helplessness in the face of stress predisposes, precipitates, and sustains gastric ulceration', *Behavioural Brain Research*, **110**, pp. 161–74.
Rescorla, R.A. (1967), 'Pavlovian conditioning and its proper control procedures', *Psychological Review*, **74**, pp. 71–80.
Searle, J.R. (1983), *Intentionality: An essay in the philosophy of mind* (Cambridge: CUP).
Searle, J.R. (1992), *The Rediscovery of the Mind* (Cambridge, MA: MIT Press).
Searle, J.R. (1999), 'Consciousness', *Annual Review of Neuroscience*, in press.
Seligman, M.E.P. & Maier, S.F. (1967), 'Failure to escape traumatic shock', *Journal of Experimental Psychology*, **74**, pp. 1–9.
Seligman, M.E.P., Maier, S.F. & Solomon, R.L. (1971), 'Unpredictable and uncontrollable aversive events', in *Aversive Conditioning and Learning*, ed. F.R. Brush (New York: Academic Press).
Selye, H. (1956), *The Stress of Life* (New York: McGraw-Hill).
Shapiro, A.K. & Shapiro, E. (1997), *The Powerful Placebo: From ancient priest to modern physician* (Baltimore, MD: Johns Hopkins University Press).
Spanos, N.P., Stenstrom, R.J. & Johnson, J.C. (1988), 'Hypnosis, placebo, and suggestion in the treatment of warts', *Psychosomatic Medicine*, **50**, pp. 245–60.
Spanos, N.P., Williams, V. & Gwynn, M.I. (1990), 'Effects of hypnotic, placebo, and salacylic acid treatments on wart regression', *Psychosomatic Medicine*, **52**, pp. 109–14.
Spiro, H.M. (1986), *Doctors, Patients, and Placebos* (New Haven, NJ: Yale University Press).
Weiner, H. (1977), *Psychobiology and Human Disease* (New York: Elsevier).
Weiss, J.M. (1972), 'Influence of psychological variables on stress-induced pathology', in *Physiology, Emotion and Psychosomatic Illness* (Vol. 8, pp. 253–65), ed. R. Porter & J. Knight (Amsterdam: Elsevier).

MENTAL CAUSATION:
FACING UP TO ONTOLOGICAL SUBJECTIVITY

Todd E. Feinberg

In this commentary I will focus on what I consider to be, from the standpoint of neurology, the most perplexing issue Velmans addresses in his paper: If the physical world appears 'causally closed', how are we to describe the causal effects of the mind? As Velmans poses this problem:

> ... if one examines the human brain from an external third-person perspective one can, in principle, trace the effects of input stimuli on the central nervous system all the way from input to output, without finding any 'gaps' in the chain of causation ... if one inspects the operation of the brain from the outside, no subjective experience can be observed at work. Nor does one need to appeal to the existence of subjective experience to account for the neural activity that one *can* observe. (p. 7 above)

This is one of the most perplexing aspects of consciousness and a primary reason for the existence of the 'hard problem'. From the objective, outside, third-person point of view, the operations of the nervous system appear to be causally sufficient and complete without reference to consciousness. On the other hand, from the subjective, inside, first-person point of view, as individuals we experience an 'inner I' that has causal effects upon our bodies and the outside world.[1] How are we to reconcile these points of view? According to Velmans:

> One simple way is to accept that for each individual there is *one* 'mental life' but *two* ways of knowing it: first-person knowledge and third-person knowledge. From a first-person perspective conscious experiences appear causally effective. From a third-person perspective the same causal sequences can be explained in neural terms. It is not the case that the view from one perspective is right and the other wrong. These perspectives are complementary. The differences between how things appear from a first-versus a third-person perspective has to do with differences in the *observational arrangements* (the means by which a subject and an external observer access the subject's mental processes). (pp. 10–11 above)

Neuroscience has made enormous progress providing purely objective third-person accounts of the neurological causes of perception and motor action. For example, accounts of the perception of the colour 'red' in terms of neural pathways and brain areas devoted to colour perception have achieved enormous specificity and detail. Indications are that we will some day fully understand without perplexity the scientific basis of colour perception. Likewise, we have causal accounts of pain perception that specify which neurotransmitters, pain receptors, neural pathways and brain regions are involved in the creation of subjective pain. It appears, at least in principle, that nothing stands in the way of a complete and non-mysterious third-person *causal* account of the neurology of pain.

When we consider the subjective first-person experiences of colour and pain the situation is less clear. While it is scientifically reasonable, from the objective point of view, to posit that the brain 'causes' the consciousness of red and pain, from the first-person point of view it is equally reasonable to claim that the *subjective*

---

[1] I have addressed these issues from the standpoint of neurology in Feinberg (1997; 2001a,b).

properties of the brain 'cause' the objective existence of 'red' and 'pain'. This is particularly clear when we consider the subjective experience of a quality such as 'pain'. While most scientists would agree that wavelengths of light, sound waves, and tangible objects exist independent of minds, 'pain' is wholly created by an experiencing subject and has no objective existence beyond that subject. 'Pain' has no third-person objective referent in the world. From the third-person point of view, c-fibres cause the experience 'pain', but from the first-person point of view the subjective properties of the brain cause the existence of objective 'pain'. Therefore, while it is appropriate to say that from the third-person perspective the activation of particular neural pathways causes and creates the perception of specific qualia, it is equally correct to say that from the first person perspective the subjective properties of the brain cause and create objective experience.

Where does subjectivity come from? The basis of subjectivity is the transparency of neural states.[2] It has been known since the time of Aristotle that the brain itself is insensate and has no conscious sensation of itself. For example, if a neurosurgeon electrically stimulates a sensory region of the thalamus or cortex of an awake subject and asks them where they experience a sensation, no subjects report that the experienced sensation is physically located within their brain. If conscious sensation is evoked, it is experienced as physically located outside of or beyond the neural system that actually does the perceiving. A person in subjective 'pain' never *objectively* experiences their own activated neurons; neurons are experienced only *subjectively*. Indeed, this can serve as a working definition of subjectivity: *subjective experience occurs whenever an experiencing entity 'perceives through' or 'acts through' a neural substrate.* Therefore, somewhat paradoxically, consciousness is created as much by what we do not objectively experience as by what we do. Sensory consciousness is created by our *lack* of objective knowledge of our own neural states, and motor consciousness is created by out *lack* of experience of the neural substrate of our actions.

For these reasons, I agree with Velmans that the brain and mind are ontologically complementary and mutually irreducible. From the third-person perspective, *mental events* have no ontological status as observable and directly experienced objects,[3] and from the first-person point of view, *the brain* has no ontological status as a directly experienced and observable object. The ontological and causal relationships between the brain and mind addressed in Velmans' article can be simply stated: *From the third-person point of view objectively observed neural states cause ontologically subjective experience for the observed subject; from the first-person point of view subjectively experienced neural states cause ontologically objective experience for that subject.*

References

Feinberg, Todd E. (1997), 'The irreducible perspective of consciousness', *Seminars in Neurology*, **17**, pp. 85–93.

---

[2] For philosophical discussions related to the subjective transparency of the brain, see Michael Polanyi's (1965a,b) discussion of the 'tacit dimension'.

[3] For more discussion of the first-person ontology of mental states, see Searle (1992).

Feinberg, Todd E. (2001a), 'Why the mind is not a radically emergent feature of the brain', *Journal of Consciousness Studies*, **8** (9–10), pp. 123–45.

Feinberg, Todd E (2001b), *Altered Egos: How the Brain Creates the Self* (New York: OUP).

Polanyi, Michael (1965a), 'The Structure of Consciousness. *Brain*, **88**, pp. 799–810.

Polanyi, Michael (1965b), *The Tacit Dimension* (New York: Anchor Books).

Searle, John R (1992), *The Rediscovery of the Mind* (Cambridge: MIT Press, Bradford Books).

THE DIFFIDENT PHYSICALIST SPEAKS OUT

Steve Torrance

Velmans offers a number of interesting reflections on how to understand 'mental-physical' interaction (particularly interaction between the conscious mind and the body). This is, he thinks, an issue which is too little discussed, perhaps because of the dominance of a reductionist or physicalist orthodoxy which assumes that mental processes (including conscious ones) are 'nothing more than' neural processes of some kind or other.

Velmans raises a number of ticklish problems to do with consciousness and causation. These include: the 'closure' problem (how can conscious thoughts affect processes in a causally closed physical world?), the 'control' problem (how can there be conscious control of processes one is not conscious of, like pre-conscious speech processing?), and the 'delay' problem (if conscious states occur too late to affect the acts they are most relevant to (Libet, 1985), how can there be any conscious volition?). Reductionists *seem* to have an easy letout from these problems: if consciousness is physical then there is no real mystery in any of these cases, they may argue. But according to Velmans, such a buyout is underwritten by an inadequate theory. Even if some form of reductionism or physicalism were to be accepted, the issues raised by Velmans would still need to be discussed.

Nevertheless these puzzles are perhaps more acute for anti-physicalists than for physicalists. Velmans has published many critiques of reductionist and other physicalist views, including an extended discussion in the first part of his recent book (Velmans, 2000). He has usefully summarized some of his key objections in an appendix to the present article. I am not convinced that Velmans has done justice to all the possible positions available to someone sympathetic to a physicalist viewpoint. Much of the present commentary will thus be concerned with the presuppositions of the discussion rather than with its internal details.

The basic package offered by Velmans to show how to deal with these puzzles is described by him as 'Ontological monism combined with epistemological dualism' (section heading on p. 10 above). When we talk about mental→physical or physical→mental causation (and, in a clinical context, the former is the domain *par excellence* of psychosomatic medicine, and the latter of psychiatry) we are, he argues, mixing two different but complementary perspectives — that of the first-person experience of the subject, and that of the third-person observation of the neuroscientist or clinician. These 'mixed perspective' ways of talking — for example invoking the way that certain practices of conscious mental imagery may affect heart rate, muscle tension, etc. — have at least practical utility 'in terms of the things that you can do (maintain that state of mind, deepen it …)'

(p. 15 above). Perhaps they are also theoretically innocent, since they combine equally valid viewpoints on the same process. But the important point for Velmans is that, while complementary, they are 'mutually irreducible' (p. 15).

I find a lot of the suggestions made by Velmans quite congenial. However I wonder whether his basic position really is immune from the some of the criticisms he levels at materialist views he rejects. Velmans distinguishes between 'reductive' and 'emergent' forms of materialist accounts of consciousness.[4] An important part of his critique of reductive theories is that reductionists confuse a number of important concepts that must be distinguished. Once these distinctions are properly recognized, he says, the appeal of reductionism evaporates, or indeed it's shown to be inconsistent or incoherent.

Thus, Velmans says, reductionists move from asserting that there are neural correlates to consciousness to asserting an identity between a conscious state and its correlate. Yet, as he points out, 'A correlates with B' does not entail 'A is (ontologically) identical with B', so the two relations should not be confused.[5] But is this fair? First: reductionists don't need to base their view on *an inference from* correlation *to* identity. They may simply argue that, given strong evidence in favour of widespread correlation between neural states and conscious states, and given the problems inherent in competing theories, asserting an identity relation seems reasonable, *in the absence of a better alternative*. (Moreover, even if 'A correlates with B' doesn't entail 'A is identical with B', the entailment does seem to go the other way, and thus identity could help to explain the correlation.)

Velmans points out that 'A = B' obeys Leibniz's law, whereas 'A correlates with B' does not. Leibniz's law is understood as saying that if A = B then all properties of A are properties of B and vice versa. But, as he further points out, there need be no such systematic property-sharing where A and B are merely correlated. OK — that's true — but if A and B are correlated *because* they are identical then of course they will have properties in common just to the extent that is required by their being identical. So invoking Leibniz's law in this way may be beside the point.[6]

Velmans further differentiates causation from both correlation and identity. Causation lacks another formal property which both correlation and identity

---

[4] See the appendix, and also Velmans (2000), chapter 3. Velmans also mentions eliminativist views which deny the reality of conscious states, but, like him, we will, for brevity, leave these out of the discussion.

[5] See appendix, p. 21–7, and also Velmans (2000), pp. 35ff.

[6] There is in any case a problem with Leibniz's law in connection with proposed mental-neural identities. Many philosophers recognize that there are important exceptions to Leibniz's law. Someone may believe Mrs David Beckham to be married to a footballer while having no such belief about Posh Spice, even though they are the same individual. Properties like '…is believed by X to have property P' — so-called 'referentially opaque contexts' — are often thought to be excluded from the scope of Leibniz's law. This may be important in getting mind–brain identity theorists out of tangles to do with failure of substitution in the case of mental ascriptions and neural or bodily ascriptions. Suppose a twinge in my knee were identical to a certain neural-bodily state S. The twinge is observed by me to be painful but S is not observed by me to be anything (since unknown to me). All such anomalies might *perhaps* be explained away by identity theorists as permissible exemptions to Leibniz's law. (But that's a big 'perhaps'.)

share, namely symmetry: if A causes B it does not follow, he says, that B causes A (indeed it's perhaps unusual for causation to be symmetrical). Velmans is right that these different relations must not be confused. But this is not enough to show why a reductionist *must* be stating a falsehood in asserting the following, for example: that for every mental state S_m there is a certain neural state S_n, such that all of the following hold: $S_n = S_m$; S_n and S_m are correlated; and S_n both causes and (in some sense) is caused by S_m.

Velmans also discusses an alternative to reductionist materialism, namely emergentism, according to which conscious states are higher-order, non-reducible properties of brains. Many of those who support an emergence view use analogies such as the relation between high-level macroproperties, (liquidity; genetic inheritance), and low-level micro-properties (the right sort of molecular structure; the relevant features of DNA). In fact, as Velmans points out, reductionists invoke similar cases in support of their view, so the debate between emergent and reductive forms of physicalism may come down at least in part to issues in the philosophy of science over differing interpretations of the same phenomena.

Velmans expresses strong reservations about any attempt to assimilate the consciousness–brain relation to cases like liquidity or to biological properties such as genetic inheritance. In this respect he follows the tradition of writers like Levine, Chalmers, etc., who see the special features such as subjectivity, phenomenality, first-person privacy, etc., as rendering any physicalist account highly problematic, if not ruling it out. Velmans believes, with them, that such special features make it impossible to assimilate the consciousness–brain relation to less problematic cases of emergence of high-level properties from low-level ones, as in the examples previously mentioned. Velmans has no objection to calling the relation one of emergence.[7] His quarrel is with the application of the word 'physical' to the case of consciousness-emergence.

Is he perhaps being a trifle unfair, however? First, he seems intent on tarring emergence-theorists with the same brush as reductionists, namely 'nothingmore-ism'. Thus he writes (on p. 26 above) that for emergentist physicalists 'consciousness is … nothing more than the higher order, emergent effect of [neuronal activity]' (and other similar characterizations occur elsewhere). Of course this is accurate, but misleading, since emergence theorists will also stress that higher-order properties, while in one sense nothing more than the effects of their constituent low-level processes, may nevertheless in another sense be *toto mundo* distinct from those constituent processes.

Also he suggests that it is just arbitrary, an act of 'relabelling' (p. 26) or of *fiat* (p. 27), to describe high-level subjective states as 'physical' emergent properties. But again I wonder if this is not perhaps unfair. For there are clearly strong arguments — to do with ontological economy, conceptual conservatism, causal closure, and so on, against introducing non-physical properties into the universe. In

---

[7] 'I should stress that I do not deny that conscious experiences can be said to "emerge" from the human brain in the sense that given brain states can be said to *cause* given conscious experiences' (footnote 20 of target article, on p. 27 above).

any case one does not have to hold to physicalism as a dogma, to be rejected only *in extremis.*

One way of describing physicalism (not a formulation that Velmans uses) is as the view that the only kind of facts that exist in the world are (in a wide sense) physical ones. In other words, if you took away the physical facts, then you would take away all the facts in the world (and *a fortiori* you would remove all the consciousness in the world). It is possible to hold such a view in one of at least two ways — either (weakly) as a view which is considered *no less unreasonable* than any competing view, or (more strongly) as a view which is thought *more reasonable* than any competing view. I think many people attracted to physicalism hold it in the former, rather diffident way, rather than in the latter way. As a weaker position, the former is correspondingly harder to dismiss than its more strident variant.

Merely saying that the presupposition that conscious subjective states are physical is arbitrary or not rationally forced upon us is not sufficient to dislodge the more diffident form of physicalism, surely, for no such claim is there being made. This kind of adherent of physicalism will concede that they do not have any conclusive argument for their view: rather, they will say, it is to be preferred for the pragmatic reasons mentioned earlier, so long as it is not shown to be inconsistent or otherwise rationally objectionable. I don't see that Velmans has pointed out any inconsistency or incoherence in the view that subjective properties are physical: as far as I can see he has merely claimed that there is no necessitation to believe it.

So I'm arguing that perhaps a somewhat self-effacing, emergentist form of physicalism may require a stronger argument than Velmans seems to want to give in order to dismiss it from the stage. (Plenty of people have advanced such arguments, of course — Chalmers (1996) is one of the most notable.) Perhaps Velmans' complaint is that such a view — he refers specifically to that of Searle (1987) — is incapable of explaining *why* the relevant macrofeatures of the brain that are to be identified with consciousness should have the subjective feel that they do have. But a diffident supporter of emergent physicalism does not, perhaps, have to see their view as committing them to supplying an explanation of why such emergent states must have the subjective feel about them (although no doubt if an explanation were to come along they would welcome it as much as anyone).

In any case, it's not clear that Velmans' own view is really that distinct from this kind of physicalism. First, in describing his position as one of ontological monism, he seems to be opening himself up to the following line of questioning: 'Doesn't monism imply unity? So are you not saying that the neuroscientist's third-person facts and the subjective first-person facts are two equally real parts of a single unity? But then, if one side of this unity is physical, mustn't the other side also be physical (or it's not a unity)?' Perhaps Velmans' answer to this is that neither the third-person physical facts nor the first-person subjective facts are ultimately real, and that the underlying bedrock of reality is neither the one nor the other. (I guess this is implied by his calling it a 'dual-aspect' theory.) Some of the remarks he makes towards the end of his book suggest this interpretation, particularly his suggestion (Velmans, 2000, p. 249) that it is perhaps information-processing that lies at the heart of both conscious experiences and their physical correlates.

But then there is a second problem: Velmans does not really express anything more than the most tentative speculation about how this duality-in-unity is to be understood or explained — merely to characterize it in terms of 'information-processing' in the way that he does seems to be merely to 're-label' it , which is to open himself to just the kind of complaint he lays at the feet of physicalists. Velmans refers to wave–particle complementarity to help make things clearer,[8] but this is offered only as a helpful analogy, and the obscurity of the idea of quantum complementarity is fully acknowledged in the field, so the help it gives is very limited.

So Velmans' own position may be less clearly demarcated from emergentist physicalism (e.g. as found in Searle) than might be thought. In so far as it is distinguishable from the latter, it may rest on some very strongly revisionary conceptions of the nature of physical 'reality'. And his complaints against some of the views he opposes may be deemed unfair if they are requiring of them a standard of clarity and conclusiveness in explaining the link between third-person and first-person manifestations of consciousness that does not seem to be available for his own view.[9]

Notwithstanding these concerns, Velmans has some important issues to raise about mental–physical interaction. The puzzles he addresses require an account on any view, and some of his positive suggestions are extremely plausible and make important contributions to the growing area of psychophysics.

References.

Chalmers, D. (1996), *The Conscious Mind: In Search of a Fundamental Theory* (New York: OUP).
Libet, B. (1985), 'Unconscious cerebral initiative and the role of conscious will in voluntary action', *Behavioral and Brain Sciences*, **8**, pp. 529–66.
Searle, J. (1987), 'Minds and brains without programs', in *Mindwaves*, ed. C. Blakemore and S. Greenfield (Oxford: Blackwell).
Velmans, M. (2000), *Understanding Consciousness* (London: Routledge).

NONREDUCTION, CONSCIOUSNESS AND PHYSICAL CAUSATION

Robert Van Gulick

Max Velmans presents and then attempts to defang several apparent threats to the causal efficacy of consciousness and personal agency. The sort of non- reductive pluralism that he proposes strikes me as plausible and very much in the mainstream of current philosophic thought on mind–body matters. It is less clear how successfully his specific replies to the alleged three threats disarm their targets.

---

[8] See footnote 13 (p. 14 above); also Velmans (2000), ch. 11.

[9] See Velmans (2000), p. 250: 'At present there is little more about 'what dwells within the explanatory gap' that can be said with confidence.' I don't deny that Velmans seeks as much clarity as possible, in a domain where the latter is desperately at a premium.

Nonreductive physicalism has been perhaps the most widely accepted view of the mind/body relation among Anglo-American philosophers for the past quarter century. The approach, as articulated by Jerry Fodor (1974) and Hilary Putnam (1972; 1978) in the mid 1970s, aims to combine a pluralist nonreductive view of theories with an ontological commitment to the physical as the underlying basis and substrate of mind (and of all else that is real). The former claim, referred to by Fodor as the 'autonomy of the special sciences', expresses the belief that describing and understanding reality requires us to use a wide diversity of theoretical, conceptual and representational schemes, many of which cannot be reduced to the language and concepts of physical science. The natural world exhibits order and regularity at a variety of levels, and we need to use a wide range of intellectual and cognitive tools to model and interact it with in its diverse aspects.

Economic cases are often used to illustrate the basic point. All economic transactions may be at base physical events, yet no one would propose that we should construct our economic models using only the language and properties of physical science. In part this is because economic facts and concepts divide up the world along lines that crosscut those associated with physical theory. There are many ways to make a thousand dollar payment, and though they are all realized by underlying physical processes, the specific properties involved vary radically from case to case. I might pay by writing a bank cheque, using a credit card, making an electronic transfer or by handing over ten one hundred US dollar bills or any other mix of currency and coins that sums to one thousand dollars. Each and every such transaction is a physical event, but they share little in common physically. What makes it appropriate to group them all together as events of a given sort is the economic regularity they instantiate within the rich social financial context in which they occur. It would be hopeless to try reduce the concepts, kinds and models of economics to those of physics or to do economics using only the linguistic conceptual tools that suffice for doing physics. Yet no one is seriously worried by a money/matter problem, nor are there any serious advocates of money/matter dualism. The theoretical, conceptual and representational autonomy of economics need not threaten the ontologically physical status of economic events.

Velmans' own view seems to be in much the same spirit, though it is unclear just how much it agrees in its actual specifics. He describes his view as 'ontological monism combined with epistemological dualism' (p. 8), and in that respect his view accords with mainstream nonreductive physicalism. Both hold that there is a single underlying reality that is legitimately viewed and conceptualized from more than one irreducible perspective. However, Velmans' position seems to diverge in at least three important respects from typical nonreductive physicalism.

1. First it is presented a matter of *dualism* rather than *pluralism*. This may well be more a matter of exposition rather than substantive disagreement. Velmans may indeed be willing to generalize his point about the legitimacy of mutually irreducible perspectives far more widely than his use of the term 'dualism' would suggest. However, that is not obvious. He may instead regard the mental/physical

distinction as special, and thus he many not want to generalize and assimilate it to all the other cases to which the pluralist appeals in distinguishing irreducible perspectives among the biological, the chemical, the evolutionary, the economic, the geological, the historical, and perhaps even the Freudian, the Marxist and the feminist. Perhaps Velmans would take such assimilation to diminish the force of his claim about the mental and the physical, or perhaps he would take it as confirming reinforcement. I cannot infer his view on this matter with any confidence based on what he says in his article. Clarification would be welcome.

2. His view seems to equate the mental perspective with the first-person perspective, whereas nonreductive materialism generally distinguishes between the two and treats the first-person perspective(s) as a subset of of a larger set of mental perspectives, some of which are quite third-person in nature and application. For example, many would take the perspective of ordinary intentional folk psychology, i.e. the rational agent perspective of belief, desire, motive and intention, to be a largely third-person perspective applied primarily in making sense of the rational purposive behaviour of those around us. Daniel Dennett's intentional stance (1987) is explicitly constructed as a third-person perspective but one that Dennett and many others regard as genuinely mental and intentional. Velmans equation of the mental perspective with the first-person perspective might seem to exclude such alternative third-person mental perspectives, or at least to deny their status as genuinely mental.

Again the disagreement may be more apparent than real; perhaps Velmans would accept the existence of genuinely mental third-person perspectives that are legitimate and essential despite being as irreducible to the physical perspective as is the first-person perspective on which he fixes his sole attention. The apparent difference may again be just a matter of exposition rather than substance. However, it is not clear from what Velmans actually says in his article, and he might indeed intend to link the mental perspective quite tightly to the first-person point of view. John Searle (1992) for example has done just that. He argues that nothing is genuinely and nonderivatively mental except what is apprehended from the first-person point of view. That view is a distinctly minority one in the current philosophic world, but it nonetheless represents a live option, and thus one that Velmans as well might endorse. The extent to which he intends such a limitation on the mental perspective remains unclear from what he says in his paper, though his willingness to include nonconscious mental factors in his account of volition and choice makes it seem that his view of the mental is less closely linked to the conscious first-person perspective that is Searle's. Once again clarification would be welcome.

3. Velmans appears not to regard his view as a variety of physicalism, which would be a significant respect in which it differs from current mainstream nonreductive views. Both Velmans and the nonreductive physicalist are committed to the an ontological monism, but while most nonreductivists take the underlying reality to be physical, Velmans seems to tend more toward some form of neutral monism or dual aspect theory. Although his position on this issue is not explicit in his article, it seems that he takes the ur reality to be neither physical

nor mental. If that is so, then he surely parts company with nonreductive physicalists. However, the reasons for doing so remain unclear. Thus it would be helpful if Velmans would clarify his position on this central issue, and give a fuller explanation of his reasons for rejecting physicalism, if he in fact does so.

At this point a dilemma presents itself. Either Velmans rejects physicalism or he does not. Whichever he opts for, he must confront the challenges raised by the critics of nonreductivism, such as Jaegwon Kim (1989; 1990; 1999), who argue that unless the mental reduces to the physical it can have no impact on the physical world and thus could not have most of the causal effects we are inclined to attribute to it. These critics appeal to the supposed causal closure of the physical world, which is the basis of the third of the three apparent challenges that Velmans himself raises against the causal status of consciousness. So it will be best to turn our attention to those specific threats and Velmans' attempts to blunt them.

He raises three apparent threats to the causal status of consciousness:

- We lack (conscious) knowledge of (the details of) the relevant processes.
- Consciousness occurs too late to effect the (relevant) processes, those to which they most closely relate.
- The causal closure of the physical precludes (any nonreductive form of) the mental from having any causal effect on the physical.

(Parentheses are inserted to emphasize key aspects of the claims which may be presumed rather than stated.) The first two of these strike me as far less threatening and capable of being answered on fairly narrow grounds without appeal to any grand or general metaphysical cum epistemological principles, of the sort which may however be needed to deal with the third.

Regarding the first, what sort of knowledge need we have of a process and of its detailed working in order to affect, control or initiate it? The answer is often very little. When I work at my computer I make use of all sorts of high level commands that are made available to me through the virtual machine interfaces that allow me to interact with the programs that I have running on it. I need not know anything about the underlying structure of the operations that execute those commands, yet I surely can and do exercise a great deal of control and influence on what happens. Similarly the causal and control affordances through which conscious experiences and thoughts are able to elicit and affect underlying mental operations are likely to involve similar high level virtual interfaces. That is, consciousness is likely to exercise its influence on mental processes through a high level, perhaps even conscious, mode of conceptualizing the nature of those processes rather through any knowledge or understanding of their underlying details. If this is so, then I think it blunts the force of the first objection. We may indeed lack conscious knowledge of the details of many of the processes that consciousness is supposed to control, but lack of that knowledge need not undermine such control as long are there suitable high level interfaces and modes of access through which our conscious states can have appropriate effects on those processes. When I consciously reason, imagine, 'move' around an imagined space, or call up remembered experiences, my ability to do so does not depend upon any conscious knowledge of how those processes are implemented or realized at the nonconscious level. All that is needed is that I can elicit or produce them through the relevant interface, just as I can call high level operations on my computer through its virtual machine commands. Thus it would seem that the first challenge to the causality of consciousness is easily met.

Answering the second, or 'too late', challenge is a matter of taking care in determining what should count as a relevant process, when it is claimed that consciousness occurs too late to affect the relevant processes, those to 'which they most obviously relate'. Velmans claims that conscious 'experiences relate most closely to those processes that *produce* them' (p. 13). More specifically he claims, 'Visual perception becomes "conscious" once visual processing results in a conscious visual experience, cognitive processing become "conscious" once it produces the inner speech that forms a conscious thought and so on. Once such experiences arise the processes that have produced them have already taken place.' I find Velmans' argument puzzling. I agree of course that conscious experiences follow the processes that produce them. How could it be otherwise? But why should that in anyway impugn the commonly accepted causal status of conscious experiences? Neither folk psychology nor any scientific model of consciousness of which I know supposes that experiences produce the very processing from which they themselves result. However that fact seems irrelevant to assessing the causal status of experience. Even if these processes are those to which experiences are 'most closely related' — which is itself unclear since I have no idea how to measure such a unarticulated claim of closeness — they nonetheless do not seem to be the processes that are relevant to assessing the validity of our ordinary beliefs about the causal efficacy of conscious experience. When I walk down the street and see a thirty percent off sale sign in a bookstore window, no one supposes the visual processing that produces my conscious experience is itself a result of that very conscious state (though it may be influenced through top down processing by my prior conscious state.) However, my conscious experience of the sale sign may cause me to recall a book I have been wanting to purchase but had deferred because of its high price. It may thus also cause me to change my immediate plans and walk into the bookstore to see if it has that volume in stock. Thus Velmans' second challenge strikes me as a seeming non sequitur. Regardless of whether the processes that produce conscious experiences are those 'to which they are most closely related', they do not seem to be those relevant to determining whether or not conscious experiences have the causal effects they are commonly supposed to have.

Perhaps I have misunderstood Velmans' line of argument here, but it does not as far as I can see pose any real threat to the commonly accepted causal role of experience in the explanation of human action.

We come at last to the third and most daunting of Velmans' three apparent challenges, namely that the causal closure of the physical seems to leave no room for conscious experiences to have any impact on the physical world, including on the physical motions of my body or the physical activity of my brain. The claim relies upon an implied nonreductive view of consciousness; that is, the claim can be read as a conditional: 'If consciousness is not reducible to the physical then it can have no impact on the physical given the closed causal nature of the physical.' If everything physical that happens has a complete explanation in terms of solely physical causes, then there would seem to be no causal work left for conscious experiences to do. The nonreductive assumption is essential to giving the challenge its bite; if conscious experiences were reducible to the physical their having effects on the physical would involve no violation of its supposed causal closure. It is thus that critics of nonreductivism, such as Kim (1990; 1999), argue that reductivism is the price one must pay if one wishes to preserve the causal status of mind and consciousness. According to such critics, it is only if conscious experiences turn out to be wholly physical events that they can have the sorts of causal impacts on our bodies, our behaviours and the rest of the physical world that they are almost universally taken to have. By contrast, they argue that any nonreductive view of mind and consciousness condemns them to epiphenomenal status and causal impotence at least with respect to everything physical. Reducibility they claim is the price one must pay to earn causal potency. This line of attack on nonreductivism, which is often referred to as the 'causal exclusion argument' (Kim, 1990), seems similar in its essentials to Velmans' third challenge.

The literature on this issue is enormous (see for example the papers in Heil and Mele, 1993), and I will not try to review it here. What matters for present purposes is that the exclusion argument is aimed at all nonreductive views of mind, applying equally to Velmans' dual aspect version as to more common forms of nonreductive physicalism. The thrust of the argument is the same against both. The causal closure of the physical leaves no room for anything nonphysical to have a causal impact on the course of physical events. Thus unless the mental reduces to the physical, i.e. unless it is in some sense really physical, then the mental can not causally affect what happens in the physical world. Unless my conscious experience of the sale sign in bookstore windows reduces in some relevant sense to some physical state or process in my brain, then it can not be even part of the cause of my turning and walking into the store to check the philosophy shelves. We need not worry about arcane and controversial cases of supposed mind/body interaction in alternative medicine. Even the most mundane and seemingly obvious cases in which our conscious lives appear to affect our behaviour would be called into question by the exclusion argument in so far as one holds a nonreductive view of mind. Or so at least the proponents of the exclusion argument allege.

What is Velmans' reply and how does it compare with those given by nonreductive physicalists? His response to the causal closure of the physical turns mainly on his epistemological dualism and his claim that the first- and third-person perspective are complementary and equally essential for understanding the nature of mind and consciousness. As indicated above, I am sympathetic to the need for a plurality of perspectives, but I do not see see how that in itself provides a reply to the challenge of the exclusion argument.

If the physical factors revealed from the third-person perspective give a complete causal explanation of physical events and nothing nonphysical can have a causal impact on the physical, then there does not seem to be any room for other factors viewed from an alternative perspective to act as causes of physical events, such as the movement of my body when it turns and walks into the bookstore. That alternative perspective might have some value and interest, but it can not do so by making us aware of nonphysical causes of the physical. The possibility of such factors is ruled out by the causal closure of the physical.

Perhaps an analogy will help. In a modern sports stadium, I might watch various game plays on the giant display screen, some of which depicted live action, some of which are show replays and some of which may be just simulations. The scenes and changes on the screen have a regularity and order that can allow for reliable prediction, but the depicted events do not in fact cause each other. The depicted ball may well sail across the screen with a speed and direction that reliably follows from the speed and angle of the depicted foot that made contact with it, but the depicted foot does NOT cause the depicted flight of the ball. Both are instead the causal effects of processing in the graphics software that generates the changing display.

The challenge posed by the exclusion argument is to give good reasons for believing that in the mental case we are not observing a similar illusion of causation. Yes, we see events in a regular and reliable order of succession that looks like mental properties causing physical effects, but the proponent of the exclusion argument claims we are mistaken. Since nothing outside the physical causally effects the physical, any perspective that seems to indicate otherwise is merely an illusion. The causal closure of the physical is inconsistent with there being any non-physical cause of my body's turning and walking into the bookstore. An appeal to epistemological dualism and complementarity by itself does not suffice to resolve the apparent contradiction. Velmans' response is a version of what is called a 'no competition' solution, i.e. one according to which the causal explanation at the mental and physical levels can both be true because they do not compete. But in order to make such a claim plausible, one needs to explain specifically how and why they do not compete and how they might thus both be true. In that respect, I do not see how the crucial details of the story are supposed to go on Velmans' complementarity view.

The problem is a serious one for nonreductive physicalists as well, but their commitment to the ultimately physical nature of the underlying or basic reality gives them an option that may not be available to Velmans and other dual aspect theorists. What makes the nonreductive physicalist a physicalist is a commitment to the physicality of all the underlying entities, properties and forces that realize or instantiate the higher level patterns and regularities that we apprehend from a plurality of perspectives quite distinct from those provided by physics and the physical sciences. Biology, immunology and evolutionary theory provide concepts and organizing structures that allow us to grasp and understand high level organizing features of the biological realm, but deep down at some fundamental level all those features are fully realized and implemented by physical structures that behave as they do solely because of their physical natures plus their mode of combination; vitalism is just false in the actual world. Thus when we view any specific instance of a higher level regularity, we are in fact seeing the world of physical reality and physical causes but through a set of concepts and cognitive structures that allows us to abstract from the blizzard of physical details to grasp robust and resilient patterns that are instantiated by that underlying physical reality.

The nonreductive physicalist is thus in a position to explain why the mental and physical causal explanations do not compete. It is simply an application of the general principle of noncompetition between mechanisms and their implementations. I can dim the lights by turning the rheostat built into the dimmer switch, and that explanation is not made false by the fact there is a more micro account that might be given of just how the construction of that particular switch increases its resistance to current as I turn it. Similarly if mental states and conscious processes are all physically realized at the underlying level, then there need be no competition between the mental and physical causal explanations one might give of my behavior when I turn to walk through the bookstore door.

Critics of the nonreductive view have unsurprisingly not been persuaded by such attempts to rebut the causal exclusion challenge by replies based on the noncompetition between realizer and realization. That sort of move, they protest, is not available to the nonreductive physicalist, since the absence of reductive links between the mental and the physical precludes the very sorts of cross level implementation relations it requires.

I believe the nonreductive physicalist can answer such charges and I have tried to do so elsewhere (Van Gulick, 1992; 1993) The story is too long to lay out here, but the goal is to give an account of the sense in which higher level regularities might apply 'in virtue of' lower level ones, despite our human inability to put the schemes we use to describe and represent the various levels into the sort of tight correspondence that traditional reductivism demands. It is thus a specific instance of the general tension in the nonreductive view between on the one hand its ontological commitment to the physical as the basis in virtue of which all else applies, and its denial of our ability to make the sorts of links between our cognitive and theoretical structures that would allow us to deduce our mental concepts and theories from our physical ones or to substitute the latter for the former in every practical application.

Resolving that tension is a challenge, but one I believe can and has been met elsewhere (Van Gulick 1992; 1993). By contrast, it remains unclear whether or how Velmans might use the his notion of complementarity to spell out the details of his own version of the noncompetition approach. He may indeed have the means to do so, but further explanation is clearly called for.

References

Dennett, D. (1987), *The Intentional Stance* (Cambridge, MA: MIT Press).
Fodor, J. (1974), 'Special sciences, or the disunity of science as a working hypothesis', *Synthese* , **28**, pp. 77–115. Reprinted in Fodor (1981).
Heil, J. and Mele, A. (ed. 1993), *Mental Causation* (Oxford: Clarendon Press).
Kim, J. (1989), 'The myth of nonreductive physicalism', *Proceedings and Addresses of the American Philosophical Association*, **63**, pp. 31–47. Reprinted in Kim (1993).
Kim, J. (1990), 'Explanatory exclusion, and the problem of mental causation', in *Information, Semantics and Epistemology*, ed. E. Villanueva (Oxford: Basil Blackwell).
Kim, J. (1999), *Mind in a Physical World* (Cambridge, MA: MIT Press).

Putnam, H. (1972), 'Philosophy and our mental life', in *Mind, Language and Reality, Philosophical Papers Volume 2* (London: Cambridge University Press).
Putnam, H. (1978), *Meaning and the Moral Sciences* (London: Routledge and Kegan Paul).
Searle, John (1992), *The Rediscovery of the Mind* (Cambridge, MA: MIT Press).
Van Gulick (1992), 'Nonreductive materialism and intertheoretical constraint', in *Emergence or Reduction? Essays on the Prospects for Nonreductive Physicalism*, ed. A. Beckermann, H. Flohr and J. Kim (Berlin: DeGruyter).
Van Gulick, R. (1993), 'Who's in charge here and who's doing all the work?', in Heil and Mele (1993).

IT'S TIME TO MOVE ON FROM PHILOSOPHY TO SCIENCE

Jeffrey Gray

The complementarity model

Max Velmans has done so much to clarify the nature of the Hard Problem of consciousness, both in his important review of the literature demonstrating the lateness of conscious experience (Velmans, 1991; see also section 3 on p. 9 above) and in his lucid overview of the whole area (Velmans, 2000; required reading!), that I am reluctant to launch an outright attack on the position he adopts. But that is what commentaries are for; so here goes.

In essence, the Hard Problem can be stripped down to just two questions: how does the brain create qualia; and how does the brain inspect them? (It *may* be possible to eliminate the second of these questions; Gray, in preparation.) I shall call these the 'central questions'. In the target article Velmans unnecessarily distracts us from the central questions by asking us to consider four possible putative routes of causation: mental to mental, physical to physical, mental to physical, and physical to mental. This division would be of serious value only if it demonstrated a new way of tackling the central questions. But Velmans does not attempt any such demonstration. That is because he believes he *already* has a solution to the Hard Problem. The four different routes of causal action that he puts under the microscope serve only to let him demonstrate this solution. That would be a useful exercise, if it were a genuine solution. But it isn't; so the exercise becomes vacuous.

Velmans' proposed solution, as is probably well known to most *JCS* readers, is a version of dual aspect theory. First-person and third-person accounts of what goes on in John's consciousness/John's brain are both correct. They deal with exactly the same information, but observed from different perspectives. Hey, presto, Houdini is out of the box! (My summary is admittedly crude; for a full account, see Velmans, 2000.)

Philosophical arguments, including those deployed by Velmans, have played a vital role in clarifying the Hard Problem. But it is time for the problem finally to come out of the philosophical closet. Conscious experience is part of the natural world. Therefore, the only satisfying explanation will be one that shows how consciousness is linked to the scientific account that applies to the rest of that world. The standard criterion for whether or not a proposed theory forms part of science is potential falsifiability by empirical observation. I cannot think of any such test of Velmans' model, nor has he proposed any himself. The same is true, so far as I know, of all other versions of dual-aspect theory, including for example

Chalmers' (1996) attempt to seek a common basis for the physical and conscious realms in an underlying stuff of 'information' (a move Velmans also makes, in his section on 'the neural correlates of conscious experience'). Thus, Velmans' proposed solution to the Hard Problem is purely philosophical, which is to say, purely verbal. It purports to tell us what we 'really' mean when we say things, respectively, from first-and third-peson points of view. We need to move beyond this.

Velmans uses the term 'complementarity' to describe his theory. First- and third-person accounts are said to 'complement' one another: both describe the same underlying information structures, and both are equally valid; but it is impossible simultaneously to take up first- and third-person perspectives towards the same information structure. The analogy with the complementarity principles of physics is clear. But the *disanalogy* is much more important. The complementarity principles of physics are embedded in a detailed theory that makes a huge array of empirical predictions, and these have passed the test of experiment over and over again. It is not impossible that a complementarity theory of consciousness may one day be formulated in a similarly testable manner. But that day has not yet come.

I am reminded in this respect of Searle's (1987) suggestion that consciousness is an emergent, high-level property of a system made up of micro-elements, none of which has that property itself in isolation. His analogy lies in the way that, e.g., liquidity is not a property of any individual molecule of H_2O, but only of water in bulk. Like Velmans' complementarity analogy, it is perfectly plausible. But proposals of this kind tell us only that there may one day be a comprehensible theory of consciousness along these general lines. They are, so to speak, 'prolegomena' to theories. They do not, in the absence of specific and testable predictions, count as theories themselves. I do not deny, however, that they are nonetheless useful steps forward — just the right kind of steps, indeed, that one looks to philosophy to provide. They set the stage for an eventual scientific theory that may fit with one or other of the prolegomena.

Voluntary behaviour

There is a second aspect to Velmans' target article which is only tangentially, if at all, dependent upon acceptance of his overall complementarity model. This consists in his account, in the final section ('Who's in control?'), of voluntary action (often referred to, more grandiosely, as the problem of free will). As Velmans indicates, in approaching these issues one must first dispense with the notion that voluntary action results from conscious decisions. This notion has been demonstrated empirically to be false in numerous experiments, of which those by Benjamin Libet, described in the target article, are justly the most famous.

To be sure, there are occasions when voluntary action does take place after, and apparently in consequence of, mature, conscious reflection. But these occasions are the exception, not the rule. They are picked out as special, for example, in the quasi-legal description of an action as 'premeditated'. Premeditation is seen as aggravating criminal action. But the *absence* of premeditation does not excuse the perpetrator from responsibility. This distinction maps pretty well on to one between: (1) decisions to act of which one becomes consciously aware only after the decision has been taken and when the action is already in course (capable still, at best, of being inhibited from proceeding to fruition; Libet, 1985); and (2) decisions to act taken consciously prior to (sometimes, a long time prior to) the initiation of any action at all. To absolve people of personal responsibility for the former kind of action would entail wholesale reconstruction of the law, not to speak of the down-stream effects upon society as a whole. We should avoid, therefore, that absolution if we can. But wanting there to be a certain state of affairs does not justify us in postulating it.

Velmans' solution to this dilemma is one with which I agree. Those actions that are not premeditated (a major part, perhaps the vast majority, of actions) are outputs of *unconscious* brain processing. But, as Velmans points out, this statement in no way implies that such actions lack the possibility of choice. The arguments he makes in elaboration of this point are cogent, correct and stand in no need of reiteration. I add here just one consideration.

Essentially, the brain is a highly complex cybernetic system, with multiple sub-systems in massive hierarchical and parallel interaction, each of which is based for the most part upon familiar engineering principles of feedback, controlled variables, etc. (see, for a recent and important statement of this point of view, Hurley, 1998). Overall, the system is built so as to control as well as it possibly can those variables that reflect the environment in which it has to survive. An important subset of these 'controlled variables' consist in those that are familiarly described as 'rewards' and 'punishments'. There is a large technical literature on animal and human learning and conditioning in which the detailed operations of rewards and punishments have been subjected to experimental and theoretical analysis. Within this framework voluntary behaviour is construed as behaviour which is readily sensitive to change by reward and punishment; involuntary behaviour, by contrast, is highly resistant to change by these means. Application of this distinction does not rest upon prior knowledge of the degree to which consciousness is involved in the relevant behavioural change. Indeed, the degree to which this is the case is still a matter of intense experimental investigation, and probably differs between different experimental circumstances.

In both everyday parlance and the legal determination of responsibility, the class of voluntary behaviour maps pretty well upon that same sensitivity to change by reward and punishment that figures in the technical literature of learning theory. In the legal case, the rationale for such a mapping is clear. The criminal law hands down punishment in order to discourage the performance of certain actions. There would be little point in so doing if these actions were not responsive to change by punishment. The law works because it deals with organisms — ourselves — constructed as cybernetic systems that respond to feedback from punishment (and of course reward) in just this way. Our choices are constrained by the way the cybernetic system that is our brain is constructed, and by the environment in which we develop and function. But they are choices nonetheless. Premeditation apart, conscious awareness of the choices is irrelevant.

Acknowledgement

This paper was written while I was a Fellow at the Center for Advanced Study in the Behavioral Sciences, Stanford University, Stanford, California. I am grateful for financial support to the John D. and Catherine T. MacArthur Foundation, Grant no. 32005-0.

References

Chalmers, D.J. (1996), *The Conscious Mind: In Search of a Fundamental Theory* (New York: OUP).
Hurley, S.L. (1998), *Consciousness in Action* (Cambridge, MA: Harvard University Press).
Libet, B. (1985), 'Unconscious cerebral initiative and the role of conscious will in voluntary action', *Behavioral and Brain Sciences*, **8**, pp. 529–66.
Searle, J. (1987), 'Minds and brains without programs', in *Mindwaves*, ed. C. Blakemore and S. Green-field (Oxford: Blackwell).
Velmans, M. (1991), 'Is human information processing conscious?', *Behavioral and Brain Sciences*, **14** (4), pp. 651–69.
Velmans, M. (2000), *Understanding Consciousness* (London: Routledge/Psychology Press).

SCIENTIFIC RULES OF THE GAME AND THE MIND/BODY: A CRITIQUE BASED ON THE THEORY OF MEASUREMENT

Sam S. Rakover

Velmans' approach (psycophysical theory and neurophenomenological laws) does not fulfill the requirements of the theory of measurement accepted by science. Therefore, this approach lacks the capability of empirically explaining his proposed three mind/body problems.

Introduction: Velmans' theory of mind/body

The relationship between our conscious private sensations, feelings, images, thoughts etc., called conscious experiences (CE), and our public behaviour transforms into various mind/body problems when we attempt to understand it in terms of the scientific rules of the game. Velmans focuses on three mind/body problems: (1) The 'closed system' problem proposes that there is no room for CE in the causally closed physical world; (2) The 'nonconscious physiological processes' problem proposes that CE cannot control physiological processes of which one is not conscious; and (3) The 'mental causation' problem proposes that CE cannot affect physiological events that precede them.

Velmans proposes a psychophysical theory that explains mental causation and resolves these three mind/body problems. This theory, which combines ontological monism with epistemological dualism, is based on the assumption that both CE and their neural correlates in the brain represent the same information. 'As each experience and its physical correlate represents the same thing it follows that each experience and its physical correlate encodes the same information about that thing. That is, they are representations with the same *information structure*' (p.12 above). These two kinds of information, the 'phenomenally encoded information and its correlated neural encoded information may be two manifestations (or "dual-aspects") of a more fundamental, psychophysical mind, and their relationship may, in time, be describable by neurophenomenological laws ...' (footnote 14, on p. 14 above).

Scientific rules of the game

I shall criticize Velmans' psychophysical theory and the fundamental neuro-phenomenological laws by employing certain scientific rules of the game that are accepted by the natural sciences and cognitive psychology. The critique is based on the following steps:

(1) Velmans' theory and neurophenomenological laws do not fulfill the require-ment for 'unit equivalency' (see below);
(2) The reason for (1) is that consciousness does not have units of measurement as with natural laws;
(3) Information cannot be the unit of measurement of consciousness;
(4) Neurophenomenological laws are not natural laws but are 'correlational laws' (see below);
(5) Velmans' three mind/body problems cannot be explained by appeal to correlational laws, since the problems demand explanations by appeal to natural laws.

Hence, Velmans' approach does not seem able empirically to explain the three mind/body problems.

'Unit equivalency' requirement. One important requirement of any scientific law or theory (such as Newton's theory of mechanics, statistical mechanics, electromagnetism) is that the units of measurements or their combination on both sides of the law will be equal (see Rakover, 1997). I call this the 'unit equivalency' requirement. To substantiate this, let us examine the law of free fall of bodies:

$S = 1/2GT^2$, where S represents distance of fall,
　　　　　　　T time of fall, and
　　　　　　　G the acceleration of the fall as a result of gravitational force.

The important point for us is this: in this law the combinations of the measure-ment units on both sides of the equation must be identical. As S is measured by distance, the expression GT^2 must also be measured by distance. And indeed, a simple algebraic calculation shows that this is the case:

distance = $[\text{distance}/(\text{time})^2](\text{time})^2$.

In view of this, I propose that a neurophenomenological law or theory does not fulfill the unit equivalency requirement. Let us examine a hypothetical law of pain behaviour (after Velmans' 'hot iron' example, pp. 17–18 above):

Pain behaviour = f(Aversive stimulus, Neurophysiological process, Cognitive process).

I touch a hot iron, my brain and cognitive processes start operating, my hand is withdrawn, and I feel pain and fear. Can it be shown that the combination of the units of measurement on the right-hand side of the pain equation is identical to the combination of the units on the left-hand side? To the best of my knowledge the answer is no.

It is not possible to take one group of measurements: heat, neurophysiological processes, and cognitive information, and another group of measurements:

subjective, phenomenological, expressions of pain and fear, and of a meaningful behavior (which is not a mere motor movement), and to show that the combinations of the units of measurements of these two groups are identical. But why not? My answer is rooted in the theory of measurement.

Theory of measurement. My major point is that psychological concepts do not have fundamental measurement units. By contrast, physics is based on the very fact that its concepts are built on such measurement units (see Michell, 1990; 1999; Campbell, 1953; Coombs *et al.*, 1970; Rakover, 1990). By such fundamental measurements physics builds various theoretical structures such as velocity, acceleration, force, work and energy. For instance, the theoretical structure entitled kinetic energy is based on the basic measurements of length, mass (weight) and time. This conceptual system represents the physical world and empirically explains it by employing explanation models such as the D-N model developed by Hempel (1965).

To exemplify this, consider the variable of length. We cannot only know if object a is longer than object b but also by how many units of length a is longer than b. If for instance a is <----------->, b is <----->, and the measurement unit is <->, then a is longer by five length units than b, and a is twice the length of b. <-> is therefore a measurement unit by whose means the length of any object may be measured. The measurement of length is an example of the procedure called 'fundamental measurement': an empirical procedure by which one determines the ratio between a quantitative property of an object and the unit of measurement of that property. This procedure sustains several important mathematical properties such as transitivity and additivity.

Can this measurement procedure be applied to psychology? In my view, it cannot. Consider the following example (after Campbell, 1953). We have a heap of 60 corn kernels. I add (or remove) 30 kernels. Without doubt, I have significantly altered the heap's weight and volume. But have I altered the taste of the corn by addition or removal of kernels? Obviously not. The addition or removal of the kernels does not alter the 'corny' taste. There is no measurement unit for taste whereby we may increase or decrease the taste of the corn, as we did in the physical case. Similarly, it makes no sense to propose that Jacob loved Rachel three and a half times in 'love units' more than Leah; and if we assume that Einstein's IQ was 150, it makes no sense to propose that his IQ equals the IQs of three imbeciles (150 = 50+50+50). (However, it should be noted that although in special cases mathematical models can be developed to generate interval and ratio measurement scales, they do not constitute a proof that natural measurement units in psychology do exist. See, e.g., Michell, 1990; 1999; Coombs *et al.*, 1970.)

Information as unit of measurement. Velmans proposes that a mental state (MS) and its correlated neurophysiological state in the brain (NS) represent the same information. Can information be a unit of measurement? My answer is no, for the following two reasons.

First, the concept of information in cognitive psychology relates to infinite psychological phenomena such as sensations, feelings, images, thoughts, contents of visual stimuli, voluntary acts and unconscious processes. Palmer & Kimchi (1986), who analysed the Information Processing approach to cognition, write: 'Mental events can be functionally described as "informational events", each of which consists of three parts: the *input information* (what it starts with), the *operation* (what gets done to the input), and the *output information* (what it ends with). By "mental events" we mean to include not only conscious experiences but all internal happenings that influence behavior, many of which will not produce any conscious experiences at all' (p. 40). Their analysis showed that the concept of information is hard to describe and to understand, and it seems to defy any attempts to define it, including the attempt to understand it in terms of Shannon's mathematical theory of information (see their discussion on pp. 40–3). In my view, even if one could apply Shannon's theory of information to different NSs, because of the above arguments, I do not see how one could apply it to meaningful contents of different MSs.

Second, there is a difference in the way observations on MS and on NS are carried out, and it seems that observations on MS (introspection) do not fulfill the scientific requirements for observation (for a discussion see Rakover, 1990). There are three requirements that a scientific observation has to fulfill. *Objectivity* requires that neither the process of observation nor the observer will affect the observed behaviour and vice versa. *Publicity* requires that all scientists be able to make the same observations. *Repeatability* requires that observations be repeatable or replicable. Clearly, while observation of NS fulfills these requirements, introspection of MS does not. Introspection of MS is private, and it is doubtful if it can be objective and repeatable. Given this, how can we test empirically the hypothesis that a correlated NS of a given MS in X's mind represents the same information that is represented by that MS? Since NS information is not a natural observable property (such as length and weight), but rather it is a trait that we attribute to NS, we have no choice but to rely on X's introspection. Hence, observation of the NS information is depended on the introspection of MS information, but introspection does not fulfill the requirements of scientific observation. (If, in this regard, Velmans' approach is viewed as an interesting version of the mind/body identity theory, the 'information-based' identity theory, then Meehl's [1966] discussion of the 'autocerebroscope thought-experiment' is most relevant. Observing his brain through the autocerebroscope, he discovered that while his visual cortex is in a state red, he sees green in 10% of the cases.)

Correlation and Velmans' three problems

In view of the above analysis, it is safe to propose that Velmans' theory and laws as well as psychology's theories and laws are not like those in the natural sciences. Instead we find in psychology 'correlational laws or theories', i.e., laws or theories that are based on an empirical correlation:

Behaviour = f(Stimulus, Neurophysiological processes, Cognitive processes),

where Neurophysiological and Cognitive processes are conceived of as hypothetical constructs. These constructs are indirectly associated with certain response-indices, such as pain that is indexed by verbal responses, heart rate, GSR, EEG, and fMRI. As such, it is not known if the indices represent the whole range of the hypothetical constructs, if they are not affected by other irrelevant factors, and if they are not task-specific. In contrast, due to the procedure of fundamental measurement, concepts in a natural law represent observations directly and entirely.

Can a correlational law empirically account for the three mind/body problems? My answer is no. First, a correlational law (an empirical generalization) itself is a target for an explanation and it is doubtful if it can play an explanatory role as do natural laws. And second, a correlational law is not an adequate tool to deal with the explanatory job demanded by the three mind/body problems that stem from the basic question of whether consciousness plays an explanatory role in a given behavioral system. (Similarly, we cannot turn a 3cm screw with a 0.5cm wrench.) To test this basic question empirically, we have to employ the following experimental procedures that are based on the requirements of fundamental measurement and of unit equivalency. We have to measure consciousness and see whether the obtained value is greater than zero, or we have to measure the other components in the system and see if their addition equals the total activation of the system. If the value is zero or if the addition equals the total activation, then the conclusion is that consciousness has no explanatory role. Otherwise, scientific work has to be continued, for example, to discover the kinds of connection among MS, NS and behaviour. (This is a very difficult task, since we are in a continuous flow of consciousness of different contents and intensities as long as we live.) Since these two experimental procedures are based on the requirements of fundamental measurement and of unit equivalency, and since a correlational law cannot fulfill these two requirements, it follows that one cannot appeal to a correlational law in order to account for the three mind/body problems. (Another problem that cannot be solved by appeal to a correlational law is whether cognitive processes are serial or parallel.)

In light of this, consider the closed system problem. To discover whether CE has an explanatory role in a particular closed system, we have to measure CE (or the other components) and see whether the obtained value is greater than zero. If the value equals zero, then CE does not play any explanatory role in that particular closed system. However, as argued above, these measurements cannot be carried out.

Similar things can be said about the problem of nonconscious physiological processes. The problem does not relate to the very fact that there are a huge number of nonconscious physiological processes. One cannot be conscious of millions of neurophysiological processes and function adaptively, and one does not become conscious of a stimulus (e.g., hot iron) at once, but only after the appropriate neurophysiological processes are activated (see also Rakover, 1996). Rather the empirical question is as follows: given an act that involves both CE and their correlated physiological events, can this act be performed without consciousness? As an example, consider automatic driving. It seems as if one does not need to be conscious in order to execute this action. But is this a valid description of the situation? I think not (actually, I hope not), since a minimum, low level of consciousness, which does not reside in the centre of the inner attention process, is probably involved in monitoring and controlling driving. However, this hypothesis is very difficult to test for the same reasons discussed above.

Finally, consider the mental causation problem with regard to Velmans' hot iron example: accordingly, the withdrawal of the hand precedes the experience of pain. The causal problem is that the consciousness of pain followed the swift hand withdrawal. But this may be only a seeming problem, since it is possible that a fast and low degree of conscious event, which is different from the acute feeling of pain, is responsible for the withdrawal (and even for blocking pain for a short time for reasons of adaptive adjustments). After all, withdrawal and pain are just two responses to the aversive situation. After all, as mentioned above, we are immersed in a continuous flow of multiple states of consciousness of different contents, durations and intensities. Once again, it is difficult empirically to deal with this possibility by using a correlational law.

Thus, I propose that Velmans' approach does not seem qualified empirically to explain the three mind/body problems.

A general conclusion

The above critique could also be directed at psychology at large. In comparison with research in the natural sciences, psychological research is limited and does not progress like physics (see Rakover, 1992). In nutshell, while correlational laws and theories deal with ordinal relation (scale) at most, the solutions to many psychological problems require explanations based on interval relation (scale) at least. Analogously, the fact that we do not see the earth as a ball does not mean that it is flat. This is not a pessimistic point of view, but rather an opened-eyed attempt to see where the methodological problems reside.

Acknowledgments

I am grateful to Mier Hemmo and Giora Hon who read an earlier version of this commentary and made important and useful remarks.

References

Campbell, N.R. (1953), *What is Science?* (New York: Dover).

Coombs, C.H., Dawes, R.M. and Tversky, A. (1970), *Mathematical Psychology: An Elementary Introduction* (Englewood Cliffs, NJ: Prentice Hall).

Hempel, C.G. (1965), *Aspects of Scientific Explanation and Other Essays in the Philosophy of Science* (New York: The Free Press).

Meehl, P.E. (1966), 'The complete autocerebroscopist: A thought-experiment on Professor Feigl's mind-body identity thesis', in *Mind, Matter, and Method: Essays in philosophy and science in honor of Herbert Feigl*, ed. P.K. Feyerabend & G. Maxwell (Minneapolis: University of Minnesota Press).

Michell, J. (1990), *An Introduction to the Logic of Psychological Measurement* (Hillsdale, NJ: LEA).

Michell, J. (1999), *Measurement in Psychology* (Cambridge: Cambridge University Press).

Palmer, S.E. & Kimchi, R. (1986), 'The information processing approach to cognition', in *Approaches to cognition: Contrasts and controversies*, ed. T.J. Knapp & L.C. Robertson (New Jersey: LEA).

Rakover, S.S. (1990), *Metapsychology: Missing Links in Behavior, Mind, and Science* (New York: Solomon/Paragon).

Rakover, S.S. (1992), 'Outflanking the body–mind problem: Scientific progress in the history of psychology', *Journal for the Theory of Social Behavior, 22*, pp. 145–73.

Rakover, S.S. (1996), 'The place of consciousness in the information processing approach: The mental-pool thought experiment', *Behavioral and Brain Sciences, 19*, pp. 535–6.

Rakover, S.S. (1997), 'Can psychology provide a coherent account of human behavior? A proposed multiexplanation-model theory', *Behavior and Philosophy*, **25**, pp. 43–76.

HOW VELMANS' CONSCIOUS EXPERIENCES AFFECTED OUR BRAINS

Ron Chrisley and Aaron Sloman

Velmans' paper raises three problems concerning mental causation:

(1) How can consciousness affect the physical, given that the physical world appears causally closed?[10]

(2) How can one be in conscious control of processes of which one is not consciously aware?

(3) Conscious experiences appear to come too late to causally affect the processes to which they most obviously relate.

In an appendix Velmans gives his reasons for refusing to resolve these problems through adopting the position (which he labels 'physicalism') that 'consciousness is nothing more than a state of the brain'. The rest of the paper, then, is an attempt to solve these problems without embracing a reductionist physicalism.

Velmans' solution to the first problem is 'ontological monism combined with epistemological dualism': First-person and third-person accounts are two different ways of knowing the same facts. This kind of reply is not new; it is, for example, a twist on the position expressed in Davidson (1970). True, there are substantial differences: For one, Davidson reconciles the tension between descriptions of events in mentalistic and physicalist language, not between first- and third-person descriptions of states; for another, Davidson actually provides an argument for his position, although to do so he assumes that there are no psycho-physical (or indeed, psycho-psycho) laws, something which we suspect Velmans would be reluctant to do. Nevertheless, they have in common the idea that the causal efficacy of the mental is not at odds with the causal closure of physics, since a mind-involving causal story is just another way of talking about the same facts that a purely physical causal story talks about.

This 'dual-aspect' approach is a popular tactic for resolving the mind–body problem, but it has some well-known problems, and it is unfortunate Velmans doesn't reply to these standard objections. For example, a frequently discussed issue in connection with theories of mental causation is the problem of over-determination (see, e.g., Unger, 1977; Peacocke, 1979). (Although usually stated in terms of a contrast between the mental and the physical, we'll translate the problem into 'consciousness speak'.) It would seem that any account that admits the causal closure of the physical, yet introduces the causal efficacy of conscious states, ends up in the unfortunate situation of having too many causes lying

---

[10] Actually, that's a big 'given': Although at least one of the present authors favours a Bohmian interpretation of quantum mechanics (Bohm, 1952), which is compatible with determinism, we both acknowledge that physical reality could very well be as orthodoxy says it is: non-deterministic. If so, there are indeed '"gaps" in the chain of causation that consciousness might fill'. One might doubt that such gaps could be present or significant in warm, massive brains, but there are several authors who argue otherwise (e.g., Beck, 1996; Beck and Eccles, 1992; Hameroff and Penrose, 1996; Hagan *et al.*, 2002).

around. If physical event P causes action A, and also the event of having a conscious experience C causes action A, then even if the physical world had been otherwise (P′ rather than P had occurred, say), it seems that A would still have occurred, since C would still have been there to do the causing. And conversely, if C had not occurred, it looks as if A would have still occurred, since P is still in place to do the causing. The problem is that this situation, on most accounts of causation, renders both P and C causally impotent. The very concept of A causing B has it that if A had not occurred, B would not have occurred.

A dual-aspect theory, it is said, allows one to resolve this problem. Since the physical and experiential perspectives are different ways of describing the same underlying reality, one cannot assume that if P does not occur, C still occurs. And, assuming supervenience of the experiential on the physical, one *knows* that if C had not occurred, P definitely would not have occurred. Thus, on an 'ontologically monist but epistemologically dualist' account, there is no problem of causal over-determination of effect.

But many have questioned whether this answer is satisfying (e.g., Sosa, 1984; Block, 1989; LePore and Loewer, 1989; Leiter and Miller, 1994): We'd like to think that our conscious states have causal power by virtue of their being the mental states that they are, not by virtue of being identical with some physical state, which itself has, by virtue of falling under physical laws, the true causal power. Simplistic appeals to a 'neutral' reality, which underwrites both physical and experiential causation talk, will not work here. There is a fundamental asymmetry between the physical and the conscious: Physical laws apply everywhere, both in situations where there is and where there is not consciousness, while the converse does not hold.[11] So there seems to be a primacy of the physical, and one must reply to the idea that it is this physical, causal reality which is always doing all the work.

This is only to mention one issue which must be addressed by any proposal such as Velmans'; there are others. For example, Honderich (1993) would seem to argue that Velmans' position cannot give a proper account of mental causation, while Kim (1993) explicitly argues that non-reductive approaches that try to do justice to mental causation end up violating the causal closure of the physical. By mentioning these examples, we are not saying that dual-aspect theories cannot be defended against them, nor indeed that such theories are not good contenders for a proper account of the relation between consciousness and the physical; but Velmans has not given such a defence, and his proposal would benefit from his locating it within the discussion that has already occurred in this area.[12]

One particular benefit of such contextualisation would be the clarification of Velmans' position itself. Although the above discussion takes the 'ontological monism combined with epistemological dualism' slogan at its word, there are

[11] This asymmetry implies that there is more work to be done than Velmans, even in footnote 14, acknowledges. Not only will there have to be laws relating the first- and third-person characterisations of a psychophysical state, but there will also have to be laws which tell us the conditions under which a state that has a physical/third-person characterisation also has an experiential/first-person characterisation in the first place.

[12] Some overviews of the positions in the mental causation debate can be found in Crane (1995) and Jackson (1996).

several passages in Velmans' text which are in tension with that phrase. For example, the 'epistemological dualism' part of the slogan is supposed to rule out the reductionist physicalism rejected in the appendix. But Velmans seems to be assuming a reductionist position himself when he discusses the neural correlates of consciousness in the light of his theory. When Velmans moves, without argument, from the representational nature of experiences to the existence of neural correlates of these experiences which have the same representational content as these experiences, he is either making a rather strong reductionist assumption, or (worse) postulating a dubious causal connection (between the structure of experience and the structure of neural states) that needs to be explained.

A general point can be made here. When people consider the proposal that computation or artificial intelligence (AI) can help us understand the mind, they often assume that this would only be true if the mind were in some sense computational. But this is to ignore a different way in which work in AI can be of assistance: by being a test-bed for our metaphysical theories. If one interacts with virtual machines implemented in computational hardware, one can come to realize that the mirroring of structure that Velmans is assuming need not hold. That is, computational examples make it clear that although level of description (aspect) Y is implemented or realized in (is an aspect of the same thing as) level of description (aspect) X, it does not follow that for every entity, structure or property referred to in Y there is something referred to in X to which it corresponds. For example, a computer can be understood as computing with sparse arrays, even though for any particular cell of the array there will likely be nothing localizable in computer hardware to which that cell corresponds (Sloman, 2001). It is through designing, implementing and/or interacting with computational systems realizing multiple levels of virtual machines that one's comprehension of the metaphysical possibilities is expanded. So, no, it does not follow that there must be neural correlates of consciousness (in Velmans' strong sense of the term), just as there are not, in general, silicon correlates of computation. (See, e.g., Hurley, 1998, for a quite different reason for believing that the structure of consciousness need not be mirrored in the structure of the vehicles of consciousness.) In assuming that there must be such correlates, it is hard to see how Velmans is less reductionist than (some of) the positions that he argues against in the appendix.

Perhaps sensing that he is falling into reductionism, Velmans uses three analogies to attempt to convince us that all is well, but they in fact make matters worse. Sameness of information structure does not mean that experiences are nothing more than physical states, Velmans points out. A video recording of a TV broadcast of Hamlet, Velmans says, has the same 'sequential informational structure' as the screen of the TV receiving that programme, and yet the videotape and screen states are 'not ontologically identical'.[13] Even if we assume that Velmans

---

[13] Surely Velmans does not need to claim that the experience and its correlate have the *same* informational structure; doubtlessly (and in the light of his footnote 9) the physical aspect of the system will typically encode much more information than is experientially represented. Thus Velmans may say (and *should* say, in order to reflect the asymmetry between the experiential and the physical) that the physical aspect must contain at least as much as informational structure as the experiential aspect. However, this proviso will not on its own answer the other objections we are making.

is correct in this claim, his attempt to make a point with it misfires, for two reasons. First, the problem was not that we had as data sameness of information structure, and this seemed to force us into monism. Rather, it seemed that Velmans could only move from the existence of informationally structured experiences to identically informationally structured physical states by assuming some kind of systematic, law-like relations between experience and physical reality. Perhaps this is not an ontological reduction, but it is an epistemological one; yet epistemological dualism is the only thing separating Velmans from the physicalist positions he rejects. It is this need to distance himself from physicalism which raises the second problem with the analogy: he admits that the videotape and the screen are ontologically distinct, yet he was supposedly defending an 'ontologically monist' position! It seems Velmans ends up with the converse of the position for which he was aiming: ontological dualism, but epistemological monism (in the sense that strong assumptions are made about 'informational mirroring').

This is not a problem which can be disposed of by simply deleting the Hamlet TV programme/video analogy, but is rather a deep tension in Velmans' position which surfaces at several points. Consider another analogy which Velmans offers to illustrate his view of the ontological relation between experience and the physical: that of electricity and magnetism. Velmans observes, in footnote 14: 'it does not make sense to suggest that the current in the wire is nothing more than the surrounding magnetic field, or vice versa (reductionism)'. But then Velmans wants to also have it that the duality implied by this observation is one of aspects, not of ontological character. This is meant to be analogous to the relation between the experiential and the physical. However, the analogy doesn't work: electricity and magnetism are not simply two ways of thinking about the same phenomenon, but two different physical phenomena that can be related to each other mathematically. In contrast, and crucially, Velmans claims that the difference between first- and third-person ways of thinking of psychophysical stuff is merely that of differently formatted ways of representing the same information. This is not what is happening in the case of electromagnetism: the electrical phenomenon is not just an aspect, a way of formatting the same information as that represented by the magnetic way of looking at the situation. There are situations where only the electrical description applies, and other situations where only the magnetic description applies. Prima facie, this suggests that there are two distinct phenomena involved; to argue that there is actually only one, root phenomenon will require further work from Velmans. The analogy is also spoiled by the symmetry of the electrical/magnetic relation, and the asymmetry (discussed above) of the consciousness/physical relation. It may be disputed which of the following is the case:

- Electrical phenomena can exist in the absense of magnetic phenomena, and vice versa; or
- Whenever an electrical phenomenon exists, there also exists a corresponding magnetic phenomenon, and vice versa.

However, in both cases, the 'vice versa' implies an ontological symmetry which is not shared by the experiential/physical relation. The only way to impose symmetry would be to assume (as others have been forced to do, e.g. Chalmers, 1996) that whenever there is a physical phenomenon, there is some experiential phenomenon, however slight or imperceptible or implausible, accompanying it. Panpsychism threatens.

The third analogy, that of wave/particle complementarity, is even worse. More and more physicists and philosophers take the appeal to complementarity as a *reductio ad absurdum* of particular ontological positions in quantum mechanics. They do not deny the veracity of the data that have led some to conclude that quanta have both wave and particle aspects; but they do deny that the paradox of complementarity is a satisfying way of accounting for that data. There are other, less paradoxical and thus more satisfying metaphysical pictures on offer (e.g. Bohm, 1952; Hiley and Pylkkänen, 2001). To say that your metaphysics of mind is akin to the wave/particle complementarity metaphysics of quanta is just another way of saying that you don't have a satisfying metaphysics, and choose instead to 'live with' the paradoxes.

So much for Velmans' first problem. His proposed solutions to the other two are relatively independent of his proposed solution to the first; we now consider them in reverse order. Concerning the third problem, Velmans concedes that in many cases (e.g., those documented in Libet, 1985), conscious experiences do come too late to causally affect the processes to which they most obviously relate (although they may have longer-term causal effects). Some might think that this would have the unpalatable consequence that many of our actions are involuntary, but Velmans' solution to the second problem shows why this is not so: non-conscious processes can nevertheless produce voluntary action. That seems very sensible, but there are other difficulties with Velmans' proposed solution to the timing problem. Specifically, it concedes too much: if we can be wrong about conscious experience playing a causal role in our decision to press a button, why shouldn't we be sceptical about its role in all action? Epiphenomenalism threatens.

A better response would be to resist the conclusion that conscious experience is not playing a causal role in the Libet cases. One could do this in two different ways. One could deny that subjects are infallibly accurate about the timing of their experiences. The fact that the subject takes the experience to be happening when the revolving dot is at a particular location on the screen does not imply that the experience is in fact occurring at the time when the dot is actually at that location — it might be happening about 350 milliseconds earlier than that. Alternatively, one could make the obvious point that conscious experience can play a causal role, even if preceded by a predicting readiness potential. For example, it might be that the readiness potential causes the experience, which itself causes the action. Any dual-aspect theory worth its salt will not be troubled by the fact that there is a neural causal account which explains our action; that is entirely consistent with there also being an experience-involving account.

We agree with Velmans that there are philosophical problems concerning the causal efficacy of the experiential which need to be addressed by any proper theory of consciousness. We also agree that some sort of monist metaphysics, such as is required to explain the relation between virtual machines (in computers, say) and the physical machines in which they are implemented, is required. Despite Velmans' efforts, however, these needs remain unsatisfied. We believe that the clinical, psychological and philosophical methodologies Velmans musters should be supplemented with and informed by experimental, synthetic AI work, in order to facilitate the acquisition of new concepts and refinement of old concepts that are required for advances in our understanding of the place experience occupies in the natural world.

References

Beck, F. (1996), 'Can quantum processes control synaptic emission?', *International Journal of Neural Systems*, 7, pp. 343–53.

Beck, F. and Eccles, J. (1992), 'Quantum aspects of brain activity and the role of consciousness', *Proceedings of the National Academy of Sciences USA*, 89, pp. 11357–61.

Block, N. (1989), 'Can the mind change the world?', in *Meaning and Method: Essays in Honor of Hilary Putnam*, ed. G. Boolos (Cambridge: Cambridge University Press).

Bohm, D. (1952), 'A suggested interpretation of the quantum theory in terms of hidden variables', *Physical Review*, **85**, pp. 166–93.

Chalmers, D.J. (1996), *The Conscious Mind* (New York: Oxford University Press).

Crane, T. (1995), 'The mental causation debate (mental causation I)', *Aristotelian Society Supplement*, 69, pp. 211–36.

Davidson, D. (1970), 'Mental events', in *Essays on Action and Events* (Oxford: OUP).

Hagan, S., Hameroff, S. and Tuszynski, J. (2002), 'Quantum computation in brain microtubules: Decoherence and biological feasibility', *Physical Review E* (To appear).

Hameroff, S. and Penrose, R. (1996), 'Conscious events as orchestrated space-time selections', *Journal of Consciousness Studies*, **3** (1), pp. 36–53.

Hiley, B. and Pylkkänen, P. (2001), 'Naturalizing the mind in a quantum framework', in *Dimensions of Conscious Experience*, ed. P. Pylkkänen and T. Vadén (Amsterdam: John Benjamins).

Honderich, T. (1993), 'The union theory and anti-individualism', in *Mental Causation*, ed. J. Heil and A. Mele (Oxford: Oxford University Press).

Hurley, S. (1998), 'Vehicles, contents, conceptual structure, and externalism', *Analysis*, **58**, pp. 1–6.

Jackson, F. (1996), 'Mental causation', *Mind*, 105, pp. 377–413.

Kim, J. (1993), 'The nonreductivist's trouble with mental causation', in *Mental Causation*, ed. J. Heil and A. Mele (Oxford: Oxford University Press).

Leiter, B. and Miller, A. (1994), 'Mind doesn't matter yet', *Australasian Journal of Philosophy*, **72**.

LePore, E. and Loewer, B. (1989), 'More on making mind matter', *Philosophical Topics*, **17**.

Libet, B. (1985), 'Unconscious cerebral initiative and the role of conscious will in voluntary action', *Behavioral and Brain Sciences*, **8**, pp. 529–66.

Peacocke, C. (1979), *Holistic Explanation: Action, Space, Interpretation* (Oxford: Clarendon Press).

Sloman, A. (2001), 'Diagrams in the mind', in *Diagrammatic Representation and Reasoning*, ed. M. Anderson, B. Meyer and P. Olivier (Berlin: Springer-Verlag).

Sosa, E. (1984), 'Mind–body interaction and supervenient causation', *Midwest Studies in Philosophy*, **9**.

Unger, P. (1977), 'The uniqueness in causation', *American Philosophical Quarterly*, **14**, pp. 177–88.

BRIDGING EASTERN AND WESTERN PERSPECTIVES ON CONSCIOUSNESS

K. Ramakrishna Rao

The target article by Max Velmans is yet another step in his continuing struggle to understand the complementarity of first-person and third-person aspects of consciousness. This struggle began about a decade ago with his first major effort in a target article (Velmans, 1991) in *Behavioral and Brain Sciences* and culminated in his *Understanding Consciousness* (Velmans, 2000). The present article, which covers the middle ground, is an instructive summary exposition of his main thesis that relates to the reconciliation of the irreducibility of conscious experience to brain states, on the one hand, and to its inalienable connection to the physical processes in the brain, on the other. In order to understand the full import of Velmans' reasoning and arguments, it is necessary to read the target article along with his earlier publications. Therefore, in the following comments I draw freely from Velmans' other writings.

His *BBS* article was generally misunderstood as espousing epiphenomenalism, even though Velmans was explicit in asserting the irreducibility of first-person conscious experience. The misunderstanding appears to stem from his assertion that information may be processed at all levels without consciousness entering into it, and that consciousness is causally inert when seen from the perspective of the third-person. The book *Understanding Consciousness* may also be misunderstood from the opposite side as tending to support the nonphysical nature of consciousness, and thus appear to espouse some kind of idealism if not dualism, even though Velmans is again forthright in acknowledging his adherence to realism and his rejection of philosophical dualism.

Velmans' views on mind, consciousness and brain may be summarized thus. Mind viewed objectively, i.e. from the third-person perspective, is the brain, its states, associated processes and observable events. Consciousness is the mind viewed from the first-person perspective, one's subjective experiences. Both perspectives represent reality. They are complementary and mutually irreducible, even though one may switch perspectives. On the one hand, our conscious intentions appear to influence our actions. Beliefs appear to have physical effects. Placebos are curative. On the other hand, (1) the physical world appears to be causally closed; (2) consciousness does not seem to enter one's own 'brain/body processing'; and (3) conscious experience seems to follow rather than precede 'brain/body processing'. The latter unlike the former appear to rule out any causal role for consciousness, a role that is experientially evident, taken for granted in folk psychology, and for which there is some credible scientific evidence. Velmans seeks to reconcile these two opposing notions about the causal efficacy of consciousness by (a) advocating the complementarity of first-person and third-person perspectives, (b) introducing the notion of perspectival switching to account for mental→physical and physical→mental causation and (c) postulating preconscious minds. These exercises are interesting in themselves, but are hardly adequate to address the main problem of the causal efficacy of consciousness. Velmans appears to commit category mistakes when he attempts to resolve ontological issues by reducing them to epistemological concerns.

One may be reminded here of a biologist–priest who teaches evolution in his college classes and preaches creation in his Sunday sermons. Obviously, he has two perspectives, one that of a scientist and the other that of a devout Christian. The two are clearly not reducible. If they were, he would not be holding them. From this, can we argue with any degree of conviction that the two perspectives of the biologist-priest are complementary and that his dual roles in the classroom and the church arise from legitimate perspectival switching?

The fundamental issue is whether conscious experience is ontologically identical to brain states. If it is, mental causation is none other than physical causation. If on the contrary, consciousness belongs to a distinctly non-physical category, then the issue of interaction between the physical and the mental arises. By accepting preconscious minds, Velmans acknowledges that minds are not limited to focal awareness. He, however, appears to be unwilling to give up the notion that consciousness is essentially focal awareness and is reluctant to extend the connotation of consciousness beyond subjective awareness.

Velmans asserts that first-person and third-person accounts are just two different formats of the same information structure. What is that information structure? The mind is stated to be a 'psychophysical process that encodes information' (p. 14 above). What is the process that encodes information from the first-person perspective? Is it also a physical, brain process? If it is, how is it different from the processes that give us information from the perspective of third-person? The notion of switching perspectives is a kind of circularity in reasoning. In order to break the circularity here, the ontological status of conscious experience needs to be expressly addressed and cannot be swept under the carpet.

To be consistent with the notion of irreducibility of conscious experience to brain states, Velmans must accept the primacy of consciousness. In order to overcome the problems he enumerates as confronting non-reductionist accounts of consciousness, he needs to draw a fundamental distinction between consciousness and mind. In the Indian tradition as represented by Samkhya-Yoga as well as Sankara's Advaita Vedanta, we find important ideas that address these issues. I tend to think that Velmans, despite his strong moorings in the western tradition, is not too far apart from the eastern perspective. I will briefly trace the common issues on which Velmans' ideas and Indian thought appear to converge, with some obvious differences.

In the eastern view as well as in Velmans' theory, our knowledge of the universe is perspectival in the sense that it is relative to the observer. It is subjective and personal. The *purusha* as the centre of consciousness is distinct and has unique experiences through its associated mind–body complex. Such observer-dependent relativity, in Yoga as well as in Vedanta, is not absolutely given but a transient condition that can be overcome by disciplined practice. The *purusha* finds itself reflected in the mind illuminating the material forms of the universe. Thus mind becomes as instrument through which the universe reveals itself. Subject–object distinction is not fundamental. It is a contingent manifestation of the mental process by which the universe is revealed. In Velmans' view, consciousness is contained in the subjectivity of data experienced. It is 'knowing what is like to see the beauty in some one's eyes, or hear the nightingale at dust is a distinct form of knowledge. It differs from abstract knowledge (or "knowledge by description") in an obvious way. . . . It is only where we *experience* entities, events and processes for ourselves that they become *subjectively real*. It is through consciousness that we *realise*' (Velmans, 2000, pp. 259–60). Thus, the function of consciousness is to confer subjectivity on data processed by our perceptual and cognitive systems. Both the views agree that the mental representations are not things themselves. Whereas Velmans is content with 'the incomplete, uncertain and species specific' representations we have of the universe, the eastern view provides for the possibility of attaining complete and certain knowledge by accessing consciousness-as-such independently of the sensory-cortical processes.

The Indian theories as well as Velmans' make a distinction between consciousness and mind. In the Indian view, the distinction is fundamental and primary in the sense that one is not reducible to the other. In Velmans' view, the distinction is secondary and holds good at the epistemological level and not at the ontological level. Thus consciousness becomes a subcategory or species of the mind. Velmans acknowledges that consciousness is not reducible to brain states or functions. Yet, he considers consciousness an aspect of the mind. The mind in his view is broader to include nonconscious mental activities as well. Here rests the real problem. Consciousness (subjective experience) is irreducible to neural states or brain functions, whereas the nonsubjective states of the mind are in principle reducible. In the light of such a fundamental difference between them, it is hardly plausible to argue that consciousness is a species or an aspect of the mind. The irreducibility of consciousness to physical states entails that the difference between conscious and nonconscious aspects of the mind is one of kind, primary and fundamental. Reducibility or otherwise of one category into another is an ontological matter and not simply an epistemological issue.

The inclusion of consciousness as a subcategory of the mind leads Velmans to equate consciousness with phenomenal data. There appears to be some confusion here between the contents and the container, between substance and form. It is not obvious that consciousness is not distinguishable from its data. Nor is it evident that consciousness is always intentional, i.e., it is about or of something. Intentionality characterizes nonconscious states as well. Conscious mentation has an additional characteristic of being subjectively experienced. Velmans agrees that experiencing the data means bestowing consciousness and subjectivity on them. The tendency to incorporate consciousness as a part or aspect of the mind is consistent with the western equivocation of mind and consciousness (Rao, 1998). This serves well reductionism, which in the final analysis leaves out consciousness all together. It is ill-suited, however, for those that accord primacy to consciousness. By regarding consciousness as a subcategory of the mind, Velmans puts himself in the uncomfortable position of limiting consciousness to a role that in functional terms is utterly insignificant.

Again, the distinction between first-person consciousness and third-person consciousness adds little to the clarity of the concept of consciousness. Consciousness is consciousness whether we look at it from a first-person or the third-person perspective. It may manifest different characteristics at different levels of observation, but it underlies all awareness. Consciousness is what makes awareness possible. It is the ground condition for all forms of awareness, like matter which is the ground condition for all the material forms we experience. Velmans himself does not seem to be excited about the notion that consciousness is something that emerged at a certain point in the evolution of the brain. Rather, he appears to favour the view that consciousness is in some primal form there from the beginning of the universe, and that evolution only accounts for the different *forms* that consciousness takes and not for consciousness-as-such. If one accepts the notion that consciousness in some form is coextensive with the universe, then it is likely that it is fundamentally different from anything that is essentially reducible to physical forms, including the mind.

The Indian views make this point emphatically and insist that the distinction between mind and consciousness is fundamental. The mind, unlike consciousness, is physical in that it can be described in material forms and accounted for in physical terms. Therefore, the interaction of the mind with other physical systems poses no special problems. The reflexivity is not between the mind with its cognitive and perceptual systems and the physical objects, events and processes. Rather it is between mind and consciousness. Consciousness does not causally interact with the mind. It has a reflexive relation with the mind. Again, the mind with its cognitive and perceptual systems is peculiarly human. The presence of mind in a rudimentary sense in other forms of life or matter in general may not be ruled out. The notion that *sattva* component in varying proportions is believed to exist in matter implies the existence of minds in less developed forms than in humans. Velmans' views appear to be consistent with the eastern accounts on this point, when he suggests that the different forms of consciousness may have an evolutionary origin, with the difference that what evolves in the Indian view is not consciousness but the mind.

Velmans as well as Samkhya-Yoga philosophers emphasize the role of the mind in connecting consciousness with the brain. I described the role in the Indian view as one of *interfacing* (Rao, 2002). Velmans' describes it as *intertwining*. There may be subtle differences between the two phrases, but they do not seem to be significantly different. However, the differences in the connotations ascribed to these two concepts, mind and consciousness, in the Indian theories and in Velmans' accounts have far reaching implications. As mentioned, Velmans seems to equate consciousness with phenomenal data. He leaves no room for possible dissociation between consciousness and contents of consciousness. The western bias that emphasizes intentionality as the defining characteristic of mind/consciousness has limited Velmans taking the next step of accepting the possibility of pure conscious experience and the existence of consciousness-as-such. If consciousness is dissociable from sensorially processed data as provided for in the Samkhya-Yoga view, all kinds of possibilities that give us knowledge of different sorts will open up. Paranormal awareness is one such form.

Velmans speaks of direct and indirect knowledge, as the Indian theories do. He points to the asymmetry of access in the two forms. We have direct access to our experiences and only indirect access to experiences of others. This seems to be so because one's consciousness is bound to and associated directly with his/her brain and not with the others. In Yoga theory, even the so-called first-person experience is indirect, because what the mind presents to consciousness are representations mediated by the perceptual and cognitive systems. Consequently, awareness arising from such mediation is also indirect. In other words, in Velmans, the direct acquaintance is with the representations, whereas in Yoga it is with the things themselves. Such direct knowledge results when the mind detaches itself from the sensory inputs and makes contact directly with the objects, events and processes in the universe. This is what may be labelled a para-normal process, distinguished from the normal process in which there is the involvement of the sensory processes. The assumption that consciousness can exist apart from the phenomenal data leaves the possibility for the existence of pure conscious states and extraordinary experiences that are not constrained by the limits of sensory processing.

In Velmans, the material universe is '*rea-ized*' through consciousness. In the Indian view, the universe is *realized* by accessing consciousness-as-such. In the former, the universe becomes *subjectively real*. We have representations that are at best incomplete approximations of things themselves. In the latter, we become one with reality and have perfect, complete and direct acquaintance with the things themselves and not merely with their representations.

In sum, Velmans took one important step forward by asserting the irreducibility of consciousness to physical states and brain functions and by pointing to the immediacy and directness of conscious experience. If he took another step to provide for consciousness-as-such and its existence apart from its contents, his views would have been a lot closer to the eastern view as represented by Yoga, Advaita and Buddhist systems of thought. Such a step would have extended his theory to account for extraordinary experiences, including the paranormal, and at the same time made sense of the eastern disciplines for culti-vating consciousness such as yoga practice that have gained in recent years a measure of acceptance in the West. Also, the additional step, it seems to me, is needed to avoid some of the inconsistencies in Velmans' account of conscious-ness and to render the distinction between mind and consciousness more mean-ingful. Moreover, his obvious enthusiasm for first-person consciousness would have been better served if he considered the possibility of separating conscious-ness from its contents. At any rate, the step he did take is a giant step for the one with a western mindset, indeed a welcome step for bridging the gap between eastern and western perspectives of consciousness.

References

Rao, K.R. (1998), 'Two faces of consciousness: A look at eastern and western perspectives', *Journal of Consciousness Studies*, **5** (3), pp. 309–27.
Rao, K.R. (2002), *Consciousness Studies: Cross-Cultural Perspectives* (Jefferson, NC: McFarland).
Velmans, M. (1991), Is human information processing conscious? *Behavioral and Brain Sciences*, **7**, pp. 131–78.
Velmans, M. (2000), *Understanding Consciousness* (London: Routledge).

Max Velmans

Making Sense of Causal Interactions Between Consciousness and Brain

Abstract: *My target article (henceforth referred to as TA) presents evidence for causal interactions between consciousness and brain and some standard ways of accounting for this evidence in clinical practice and neuropsychological theory. I also point out some of the problems of understanding such causal interactions that are not addressed by standard explanations. Most of the residual problems have to do with how to cross the 'explanatory gap' from consciousness to brain. I then list some of the reasons why the route across this gap suggested by physicalism won't work, in spite of its current popularity in consciousness studies. My own suggested route across the explanatory gap is more subterranean, where consciousness and brain can be seen to be dual aspects of a unifying, psychophysical mind. Some of the steps on this deeper route still have to be filled in by empirical research. But (as far as I can judge) there are no gaps that cannot be filled — just a different way of understanding consciousness, mind, brain and their causal interaction, with some interesting consequences for our understanding of free will. The commentaries on TA examined many aspects of my thesis viewed from both Western and Eastern perspectives. This reply focuses on how dual-aspect monism compares with currently popular alternatives such as 'nonreductive physicalism', clarifies my own approach, and reconsiders how well this addresses the 'hard' problems of consciousness. We re-examine how conscious experiences relate to their physical/functional correlates and whether useful analogies can be drawn with other, physical relationships that appear to have dual-aspects. We also examine some fundamental differences between Western and Eastern thought about whether the existence of the physical world or the existence of consciousness can be taken for granted (with consequential differences about which of these is 'hard' to understand). I then suggest a form of dual-aspect Reflexive Monism that might provide a path between these ancient intellectual traditions that is consistent with science and with common sense.*

Journal of Consciousness Studies, **9**, No. 11, 2002, pp. 69–95

I would like to thank the commentators on TA for their many excellent commentaries. To simplify the process of relating these commentaries and my replies to the original text, I will deal with them according to topic in the sequence that these topics are treated in TA. At various points I refer to more detailed treatments of the issues addressed in my recent book *Understanding Consciousness* (2000). A few of the commentaries elaborate on TA and do not require a response. **John Kihlstrom** for example gives an excellent review of the evidence for the causal effects of consciousness on body/brain, the explanandum of TA, and **Todd Feinberg** outlines an independently arrived at but similar understanding of consciousness/brain interactions to my own. Of necessity, the bulk of my response is reserved for those who challenge aspects of my analysis, seek clarification, or defend alternative analyses.

Can Reductive Physicalism Be Defended?

The causal interactions between consciousness and brain could be easily explained, at least in principle, if consciousness were *nothing more than* a state of the brain. But, in the Appendix to TA I have given some of my reasons for doubting that science will ever demonstrate human phenomenal consciousness (C) to be nothing more than a state of the brain (B). I accept the widely held view that for any given a given conscious experience there will be associated physical causes and correlates within the brain. However, causation and correlation are not ontological identity. Identity is symmetrical (If B = C, then C = B) and obeys Leibniz's law (if B = C, then all the properties of B must also be the properties of C and vice-versa). Correlation is symmetrical (if B correlates with C, then C correlates with B) but it does not obey Leibniz's Law. Causation is neither symmetrical nor obeys Leibniz's Law. Why does this matter? Suppose that third-person science had established a perfect 1:1 correlation between a given experience C and its physical correlates B. Wouldn't that suffice to establish a reductive identity between them? No, because major differences between the first-person *phenomenal* properties of C and the third-person *physical* properties of B would remain.[1] C and its correlate B would of course be intimately related. But an 'intimate relationship' need not be a reductive identity. According to dual-aspect theory, B and C are complementary aspects of mind-itself. This would explain both their perfect correlation and their phenomenal differences. So it would provide a better fit to the available facts.

In defence of a 'diffident physicalism' **Torrance** argues that *if* C and B were identical, that would also explain their correlation and 'given the problems inherent in competing theories, asserting an identity relation seems reasonable, *in the absence of a better alternative*'. Given its better fit to the available facts, I would

---

[1] As **Torrance** points out [footnote 6, p. 38 above), some philosophers have tried to defend identity theory by arguing that Leibniz's law does not apply to 'referentially opaque contexts'. I might have a twinge in my knee and just not know it to be identical to neural-bodily state S, so I might conclude that they are not identical even though they are. Torrance is cautious about this argument and I share his caution. In some future state of neuroscience we can envision having a given experience C, knowing *all* about its physical correlates B, and still not being convinced of their identity (given Leibniz's law).

argue that dual-aspect theory does provide a better alternative and that its so-called problems are not problems at all (see below). I suspect that, on reflection, **Torrance** would agree that if physicalism can only establish consciousness/brain identity by *assuming* it, then it is on very weak ground indeed.

Can Nonreductive Physicalism Be Defended?

Of the physicalist theories, those of the emergent variety are perhaps the most plausible. It is obvious that higher-order physical properties emerge from the brain's micro-operations. In a sense, conscious experiences also emerge from the brain (in the sense that brain states can be said to cause or correlate with conscious experiences). I nevertheless resist the view that conscious experiences are just higher-order *physical* states of the brain. Higher order physical states of the brain are likely to correlate with given conscious experiences, but this does not warrant a reduction of the experiences to their correlates for the reasons outlined in the section above. **Torrance** suggests that it is a little unfair to tar the emergentists with the same brush as the reductionists. Emergentists accept that what emerges may be *toto mundo* distinct from the processes that have produced them. I agree, and I also agree that there is no problem about treating higher-order emergent properties of the brain as physical if, on commonly accepted criteria, they *are* physical (e.g. the electrical and magnetic fields detected by EEG and MEG). On the other hand, if, on commonly accepted criteria, conscious experiences would be categorized as mental as opposed to physical, then calling them 'physical' becomes a mere relabelling exercise. To give this exercise bite, one would have to show that all the properties that that are normally thought of as 'mental' (first-person properties) are *in fact* physical (third-person properties) otherwise one is simply left with all the problems of why 'what it is like to be something' should emerge from or have a causal influence on the physical world. **Torrance** argues that a weak or wide form of physicalism might nevertheless be coherent and at the very least, tenable (in spite of there being no strong case for it). That may be so. But a physicalism that weak and wide would be empty. All the puzzles of consciousness would simply slip through its net.

In defence, **Torrance** suggests that there are other reasons 'to do with ontological economy, conceptual conservatism, causal closure, and so on, against introducing non-physical properties into the universe'. I accept that ontological economy (simplicity) is desirable, but it has to be balanced against *sufficiency*, and I would argue that ontological monism combined with epistemological dualism achieves that fine balance. I don't agree that conceptual conservatism should be the order of the day when we are faced with a theoretical orthodoxy about the nature of conscious experience that is so clearly at odds with our actual conscious experience. In any case, the explanatory system in *Understanding Consciousness* does have causal closure as far as I can tell. Crucially, I am *not* 'introducing non-physical properties into the universe'. I am merely suggesting another way to make sense of the phenomenal properties that are observed to be there.

Can Nonreductive Physicalism Be Defended Against My Three Threats to the Third-Person Causal Status of Consciousness?

1. We lack conscious knowledge of the details of the processes that we are supposed to consciously control. According to **Van Gulick** this does not trouble nonreductive physicalism. As he notes, we often need very little knowledge of a process and of its detailed workings in order to affect, control or initiate it. Use of a computer for example does not require one to know anything about the underlying structure of the operations that execute its commands in machine language. Yet the high level control that we exercise is surely conscious. I agree — and I have used a similar argument to defend my own dual-aspect analysis of causality in TA (p. 17 above). However, I think we need to be precise about the *sense* in which such 'conscious control' can be 'conscious'. Control can be conscious in the sense that we are conscious *of* exercising control in this high level (global) way, and for everyday purposes this experience of being in control is veridical (when we think we have voluntary control, we usually do — see discussion of free will in TA). Controlled processing can also be conscious in the sense that it *results* in a conscious experience. The critical issue, however, is whether first-person conscious phenomenology *actually* controls or *enters into* physical processing, which seems to contravene the principle that the physical world is causally closed.

2. The problem of causal closure. If first-person experiences are invariably accompanied by distinct physical correlates, and if the physical world is causally closed, I don't see how such experiences *could* exercise causal control — as the relevant control would already be exercised by their physical correlates (see the problem of 'overdetermination' raised in the commentary by **Chrisley & Sloman**). The only escape route for 'nonreductive physicalism' is to argue that, one day, science will establish conscious experiences to be nothing more than their physical correlates. As I have argued in the Appendix of TA, however, third-person science is restricted to establishing the neural causes and correlates of experiences. Given that causes and correlates are not identities, this scientific route to establishing a reductive identity is blocked.[2]

3. Consciousness comes too late to affect the processes to which it most closely relates. Scientific claims for the causal efficacy of consciousness are typically based on contrastive analysis. Psychologists commonly contrast preconscious or nonconscious processing of a given type (e.g. preconscious visual processing of input) with conscious processing of the same type (e.g. visual processing where one becomes conscious of input) and then attribute any functional differences between these to the operation of consciousness. In Velmans (1991) I pointed out the fallacy of such attributions. Conscious experiences are a consequence of

---

[2] Note that this block to establishing the ontological identity of conscious states with correlated physical states applies irrespective of the level of organisation of the physical states. That is, the block applies just as much to so-called 'nonreductive physicalism' as it does to old-style reductive physicalism. Given this, it is not obvious how **Van Gulick's** suggestion that 'higher level regularities might apply "in virtue" of lower level ones' would actually resolve the problem of causal closure.

sophisticated, focal-attentive processing and without focal-attentive processing many forms of complex, novel functioning would not occur. However, the experiences themselves emerge too late to affect that processing. **Van Gulick** asks 'But why should this impugn the commonly accepted causal status of consciousness? Neither folk psychology nor any scientific model of consciousness of which I know supposes that experiences produce the very processing from which they themselves result.' This misses my point. *Once it is pointed out* that consciousness results from a given process, of course no sensible person would claimit to have a causal role in that process. However, as far as I know, prior to my 1991 *BBS* target article, no one had pointed this out, claims for the causal efficacy of consciousness based solely on nonconscious/conscious contrasts were legion, and they continue, unabated to this day (see e.g. Baars *et al.*, 2002). I accept, of course, that consciousness might in principle enter into processing that *follows* its emergence. However, this proposal still has to surmount the problem that the physical world is causally closed (see TA, note 17 — and discussion above).

Points of Clarification On My Own Theory

Van Gulick asks whether my own view is just a variant of a form of nonreductive physicalism that accepts explanatory pluralism. This would allow higher-level forms of mental organisation to have properties that are best described at that level rather than in the more basic terms of physics, without doubting that such properties are ultimately physical. This applies, for example, to economics. No one is worried by a money/matter problem or seriously advocates money/matter dualism. So why could the same not be true of mind? **Van Gulick** also points out that my epistemology in TA is presented as first- versus third-person *dualism* rather than *pluralism* although he notes that this may well be more a matter of exposition rather than substantive disagreement.

As it happens, these issues interconnect. Rather than *contrasting* epistemological dualism with epistemological pluralism, in my own work I *combine* these. That is, I support the view that there are many forms and levels of explanation within *both* first- and third-person accounts. As **Van Gulick** notes, pluralism is commonplace in third-person science, with well-defined hierarchies defined by the size and level of organisation of the phenomena, typically ranging from microphysical, macrophysical, chemical, biological, neurophysiological, cognitive/functional, and social levels of organisation. Nonreductive physicalism usually identifies conscious experience with just one level of this hierarchy, typically the cognitive/functional level that, in turn, supervenes on the brain's neurophysiology. In my view this is an oversimplification. Like the forms of material organisation that they accompany, first-person experiences can be described at different levels and may have an ontology at different levels. Some experiences appear to be socially determined, being, in part, social constructions grounded in culture and history (e.g. what it is like to be the Prince of Wales). Others (such as empathy) are quintessentially interpersonal, requiring the presence of at least one other human being (see readings in Thomson, 2001, *Between Ourselves*). Yet others, such as visual and auditory percepts appear to be largely individual, resulting from the binding of sensory features within an integrated human brain. Under appropriately controlled conditions these features can be further decomposed into the minimally discriminable phenomenal differences studied by psychophysics and so on.[3]

It is important to note that so-called 'nonreductive physicalism' *is* reductive in that it claims conscious experiences to be *nothing more than* a form of higher order material organisation or cognitive functioning. While dual-aspect theory accepts that every distinct experience has a distinct set of third-person physical and/or functional *correlates* (at social, personal or subpersonal levels of organisation) it resists the physicalist suggestion that such conscious experiences are reducible to their correlates at *any* of these levels. Rather, first person accounts of experience and third person accounts of accompanying physical functioning remain complementary and mutually irreducible, *whatever the level of organisation*.

This brings us to **Van Gulick's** Point 2. Do I equate the mental perspective with the first-person perspective? No. Like nonreductive physicalism, I treat the first-person perspective(s) as a subset of a larger set of mental perspectives, some of which are entirely third-person in nature, for example, those aspects of mental functioning described in cognitive psychological accounts of the mind.[4] Unlike nonreductive physicalism, however, I argue that mental processes that have a conscious phenomenology cannot be *exhaustively* described in third person terms. While it is possible to describe what people *do* or how their brains function when they have beliefs, desires, etc., in third-person terms, without reference to their first-person perspective it is not possible to describe what they *experience*. I have given some of my initial reasons for the irreducibility of first- to third-person accounts in the Appendix to TA. As **Van Gulick** does not take issue with this preliminary analysis I will not offer a deeper defence of it here. Interested readers will find a far more extensive analysis in chapters 3, 4 and 5 of Velmans (2000). See also my debate with Dan Dennett in Velmans (2001).

This brings us conveniently to **Van Gulick's** point 3. As he notes, I share the physicalist commitment to ontological monism, but my dual-aspect view takes the ur reality (the nature of mind in this case) to be neither physical nor mental. Why? Precisely because it has *both* of these mutually irreducible, first- and third-person aspects. Viewed from the outside, the operations of ur mind appear to be operations of brain. Viewed from a first-person perspective, the operations of ur mind appear to be conscious experiences. Which is it really? If one assumes (as I do) that *neither* perspective is necessarily illusory or deluded, then the

---

[3] Whether more primitive forms of material organisation are associated with more primitive forms of conscious experience is a separate (controversial) issue that we need not address here. Panpsychists such as Penrose and Hameroff for example suggest that even microphysical events are associated with primitive experiences.

[4] In Velmans (1990a) for example, I defend the conventional cognitive view that many mental states are unconscious and take issue with Searle's (1990) 'connection principle' which explicitly links the criterion for being mental to being potentially conscious.

nature of ur mind must support *both* the views that we have of it. Given this, its nature is better described as 'psychophysical' than 'physical'.

This also addresses **Torrance's** suggestion that my position is not really all that different from nonreductive physicalism. He asks, 'Doesn't monism imply unity? So are you not saying that the neuroscientist's third person facts and the subjective first-person facts are two equally real parts of a single unity? But then, if one side of this unity is physical, mustn't the other side also be physical (or it's not a unity)?' He then guesses correctly that, 'Perhaps Velmans' answer to this is that neither the third-person physical facts nor the first-person subjective facts are ultimately real, and that the underlying bedrock of reality is neither the one nor the other. (I guess this is implied by his calling it a "dual-aspect" theory.)'

Viewing the mind-itself as psychophysical rather than physical is more than a simple relabelling exercise. What does this form of dual-aspect monism buy us? As I have argued in *Understanding Consciousness*:

> If consciousness and its physical correlates are actually complementary aspects of a psychophysical mind, we can close the 'explanatory gap' in a way that unifies consciousness and brain while preserving the ontological status of both. It also provides a simple way of making sense of all four forms of physical (P) and mental (M) causal interaction. Operations of mind viewed from a purely external observer's perspective (P→P), operations of mind viewed from a purely first-person perspective (M→M), and mixed-perspective accounts involving perspectival switching (P→M; M→P) can be understood as different views (or a mix of views) of a single, psychophysical information process, developing over time. In providing a common psychophysical ground for brain and experience, such a process also provides the 'missing link' required to explain psychosomatic effects (Velmans, 2000, p. 251; see also TA page 14).[5]

Escape from the problem of causal closure. In **Van Gulick's** words 'If the physical factors revealed from the third person perspective give a complete causal explanation of physical events and nothing nonphysical can have a causal impact on the physical, then there does not seem to be any room for other factors viewed from an alternative perspective to act as causes of physical events.' I agree. But we are not interested here in purely physical events. We are interested in the nature of mind, and according to the above, the nature of mind is psychophysical. Unlike 'nonreductive physicalism' this analysis of mind and M→P causation is genuinely nonreductive. And it is this that makes it immune to Kim's (1999) point that, if the physical world is causally closed, either the mental reduces to the physical, or it must be epiphenomenal. Unlike 'nonreductive

---

[5] This also addresses **Chrisley & Sloman's** point that, 'We'd like to think that our conscious states have causal power by virtue of their being the mental states that they are, not by virtue of being identical with some physical state, which itself has, by virtue of falling under physical laws, the true causal power.' Indeed! And that is yet another reason for rejecting any version of physicalism. In the above analysis, conscious experiences are *not* identical to (correlated) physical states. Nor do they 'supervene' on physical states (with the implication that the latter are ontologically more basic). They are first-person manifestations of the operations of our own psychophysical minds. They have causal powers in the sense that any phenomena can have causal powers. Although they only represent the operations of mind-itself (ur mind), from a first-person perspective we can take them to *be* the operations of mind.

physicalism' I do not claim that first-person experiences somehow enter into third-person physical functioning, so I do not need to reduce these experiences to physical events to make good that claim. Within dual-aspect theory there is a more intuitively plausible option. If the mind is genuinely psychophysical, then an entirely third-person physical view of it gives only a partial view of both its nature and its causal operations. Brain states are genuine phenomena (manifestations of ur mind), viewable from a third-person perspective, but conscious experiences are also genuine phenomena (manifestations of ur mind) viewable from a first-person perspective. Descriptions of brain states can be used to give a detailed account of the operations of mind in terms of its physical manifestations. Descriptions of first-person experience can be used to give an account of the operations of mind in terms of its conscious manifestations. For scientific purposes, third-person accounts are more useful. For everyday purposes, first-person accounts are often more useful. Both are required for an account of mind to be complete.[6]

In What Sense Does This Complementary Perspectives Account Advance Our Understanding of the 'Hard Problems' of Consciousness?

In *Understanding Consciousness* and prior work I have argued that some of the problems of consciousness require conceptual advance, some require empirical advance, and some require both. Empirical questions include, 'What are the necessary and sufficient conditions for consciousness in the human brain?' and 'What are the neural correlates of consciousness?' Questions such as 'What is consciousness?' 'What is the function of consciousness?' and 'How can one make sense of the causal interactions of consciousness and brain?' appear to be largely conceptual. Why? Because the considerable evidence that one can already bring to bear on these questions somehow fails to address them. Each and every one of us has a vast reservoir of conscious experience. Gathering more of it won't clarify what consciousness is. Extensive contrastive analyses of 'conscious' versus 'nonconscious' processing have already been carried out in psychological science. These illustrate functional differences between processes that either are, or are not accompanied by phenomenal consciousness. But such contrasts don't reveal what the conscious phenomenology itself does (see TA). Nor does the massive evidence for mind/body interactions reveal how to make sense of the causal interactions of consciousness and brain. It is the opacity of these questions to further data gathering that makes them 'hard'.

The present TA deals only with the last of these 'hard problems' (I deal with the other problems and with how they all interconnect in *Understanding Consciousness*). According to **Gray**, however, these problems are tangential to the *real* hard problem. Rather, 'the Hard Problem can be stripped down to just two questions: how does the brain create qualia; and how does the brain inspect them?' It will be apparent that I do not entirely agree. These two questions are

---

[6] The need to have *both* first- and third-person accounts for a complete account of mind makes it clear why such accounts do not face the problem of 'overdetermination' (see **Chrisley & Sloman**).

two of many. As it happens, they have third-person aspects that are fully amenable to empirical research. One proper answer to the question 'How does the brain produce qualia?' would be to specify the *necessary and sufficient physical conditions* in the brain for the appearance of conscious qualia. This can be investigated by contrasting physical conditions that are necessary and sufficient for the appearance of qualia with those that are not — a standard method in science. Viewed in third-person terms, 'how the brain inspects qualia' can be explained in terms of 'how it inspects representations at the focus of attention', 'make them available for report', and so on.

One might object, of course, that such third-person accounts don't answer the right question. The hard problem is not how one part of the brain might inspect and report on information in another part of the brain. It is how a *physical* brain could 'inspect' a first-person conscious experience! But this is precisely the question that I *do* address! Ontological monism combined with epistemological dualism makes it clear that one can give a 'pure third person account' of brain functioning (in terms of how subsystems in the brain inspect representations at the focus of attention). One can also give a 'pure first-person account' of what is going on (in terms of the way that I, a conscious being, can inspect my own conscious experience). An account of 'how the brain inspects its conscious experience' can then be seen to be a 'mixed-perspective account, involving perspectival switching' (see TA). As **Gray** notes, 'the only satisfying explanation will be one that shows how consciousness is linked to the scientific account that applies to the rest of that world.' In broad terms, that is what this analysis achieves.

Gray objects that, 'The standard criterion for whether or not a proposed theory forms part of science is potential falsifiability by empirical observation. I cannot think of any such test of Velmans' model, nor has he proposed any himself. The same is true, so far as I know, of all other versions of dual-aspect theory, including for example Chalmers' (1996) attempt to seek a common basis for the physical and conscious realms in an underlying stuff of "information" (a move Velmans also makes, in his section on "the neural correlates of conscious experience"). Thus, Velmans' proposed solution to the Hard Problem is purely philosophical, which is to say, purely verbal. It purports to tell us what we 'really' mean when we say things, respectively, from first-and third-person points of view. We need to move beyond this' (pp. 49–50 above). **Rao** also makes a similar complaint, when he suggests that I try to 'resolve ontological issues by reducing them to epistemological ones' (p. 64).

I accept the point that *some* aspects of my analysis have to do with how to understand 'what we 'really' mean when we say things, respectively, from first-and third-person points of view', namely my account of perspectival switching, and mixed-perspective explanations. However the ontological monism, combined with epistemological dualism that underpins this analysis is not just linguistic philosophy. It is a claim about the basic ontology of mind, its manifestations, and about how we can know its nature and its manifestations. For example, the proposal that first- and third-person perspectives of the mind are complementary and mutually irreducible is a claim about mind and how we can know it in the same sense that wave-particle complementarity is a claim about the nature of light, or electromagnetic energy is a claim about the unified nature of electricity and magnetism.

I also accept that my global analysis of how to make sense of the causal relations of consciousness and brain is not a theory about the *details* of how information encoded in the brain is mapped into conscious phenomenology. However such details can, in principle, be settled by empirical research, which makes them so-called 'easy' problems rather than 'hard' ones. To make sense of the hard problems we need to *think* about them in a different way (perhaps in the way that I suggest). But that does not make my *entire analysis* unfalsifiable, and purely 'verbal and philosophical'. [7] A quick revisiting of my case for dual-aspect theory and my critique of alternative theories will confirm that they are tightly linked to falsifiable, experimental and clinical evidence — to evidence of mind/body interactions (see **Kihlstrom**), to evidence that the physical world is causally closed, to evidence that phenomenal consciousness comes too late to affect the processes to which it most closely relates (Velmans, 1991), to evidence of pre-conscious and unconscious processing, and so on. Crucially, unlike the variants of physicalism and functionalism defended by **Torrance**, **Van Gulick**, and **Chrisley & Sloman**, the dual-aspect theory developed in TA also conforms closely to the *evidence of first-person experience*.

It is instructive to dwell on this last point. Although the dual-aspect analysis in TA, and the Reflexive Monism that underpins it in *Understanding Consciousness* are broad theories about how to make sense of the relation of consciousness to brain rather than theories about the neurophenomenological details, they are first and foremost *empirical* theories that try to make sense of the combined third- and first-person evidence. If there were convincing third- or first-person evidence that challenges some aspect of these theories, or some clear flaw in how the analyses connect to the data, then I would modify or abandon the theories. Many experimental and theoretical developments could challenge the details of my analysis, for example current attempts to demonstrate that a cognitive unconscious does not exist (Perruchet & Vinter, 2003), or that 'qualia' do not exist (see debate with Dennett in Velmans, 2001), or that the neural correlates of consciousness are *not* representational states that encode identical information (**Chrisley & Sloman** — see below), or that consciousness is actually a mental field that influences the activities of brain (Libet, in press). I would also abandon my 'complementary perspectives' analysis if our everyday insights into the operations of our own minds based on our first-person experiences turned out to be largely wrong.

Compare this with physicalism. Physicalism draws its scientific respectability from its namesake 'physics'. However physicalism is a philosophical thesis about the ontological nature of conscious experience, not a field of science. Its claim that first-person phenomenology reduces, without remainder, to states of

---

[7] Note that falsifiability is *one* useful criterion of a good scientific theory, but it is not an infallible criterion or the only criterion (other tests include verifiability, explanatory elegance, simplicity, sufficiency, productivity and so on). See Chalmers (1992) for a useful introduction.

the brain has no real evidence in its favour (neural causes and correlates are not identities), and massive evidence to the contrary (conscious phenomenology does not resemble brain states). This makes it basically a *faith* in the all-encompassing nature of third-person science — a commitment to a worldview that is immune to falsifying evidence. If one is looking for an unfalsifiable theory, here it is.

How Conscious Experiences Relate to their Physical/Functional Correlates

At present, we know little about the physical nature of the correlates of conscious experiences. Nevertheless, in *Understanding Consciousness* and TA I suggest that there are three plausible, functional constraints imposed by the phenomenology of consciousness itself. Normal human conscious experiences are representational (phenomenal consciousness is always of something). Given this, it is reasonable to assume that the neural correlates of such experiences are also representational states. For a given physical state to be the correlate of a given experience it is also plausible to assume that it represents the *same* thing (otherwise it would not be the correlate of *that* experience). Finally, for a physical state to be the correlate of a given experience, it is reasonable to suppose that it has the same 'grain'. That is, for every discriminable attribute of experience there will be a distinct, correlated, physical/functional state. As each experience and its physical correlate represents the same thing it follows that each experience and its physical correlate encodes the same information about that thing. That is, they are representations with the same *information structure*.[8] I also point out that different representational systems employing different formats can encode *identical information* without themselves being identical. Neural correlates, for example, might *function* as representations (encoding identical information to that displayed in their correlated phenomenology) without 'mirroring' that conscious phenomenology in any obvious physical sense. While such correlates *might* be iconic, they could also be propositional, feature sets, prototypes, procedural, localised, distributed, static, dynamic or whatever. The operations on them might also be formal and computational, or more like the patterns of shifting weights and probabilities that determine the activation patterns in neural networks (TA, note 10).[9]

Given that I do give a supporting case for this in TA (and a far more detailed case in Velmans, 2000, pp. 236–51) it is hard to understand **Chrisley & Sloman**'s contention that I 'move without argument, from the representational

---

[8] **Chrisley & Sloman** suggest (footnote 13, on p. 60 above) that I should say that 'the physical aspect must contain at least as much information structure as the experiential aspect' rather than claiming them to have 'identical information' as the physical aspect will typically encode more information than the experiential aspect. I do not deny that the brain encodes far more information than that which is manifest in conscious experience, or that this information may support the formation and functioning of the correlates of experience. However, information encoded in the brain that is not encoded in experience is not, in the strict sense that I intend, a 'correlate' of that experience.

[9] As **Chrisley & Sloman** point out, it important to distinguish the functions that are implemented by a system from the methods it uses to implement those functions. They present this as an issue on which we disagree, suggesting that a strong phenomenal experience/neural correlate 'mirroring' is implicit in my analysis. But, as should have been clear from TA note 10, this is actually an issue on which we agree.

nature of experiences to the existence of neural correlates of these experiences which have the same representational content as these experiences.' Nor is it easy to make sense of their claim that I am 'either making a rather strong reductionist assumption, or (worse) postulating a dubious causal connection (between the structure of experience and the structure of neural states).' As I have noted, different representational systems can encode identical information *without* the systems reducing to each other — and the relation between experiences and their physical correlates is, by definition, correlation not causation.

Would the Discovery of Psychophysical Correlations Be Scientifically Useful?

As noted above, even perfect 1:1 correlations between conscious states and physical states would not establish their ontological identity. It is also well accepted in science that correlation does not establish causation. Consequently, even exact neurophenomenological laws that chart the way that given physical correlates map onto given conscious experiences would not be causal laws. If such bridging laws could be found they might nevertheless document invariant, empirical relationships in a precise way — and few, I suspect, would doubt that this would be a major scientific advance. **Rakover**, however, disagrees. According to him, 'correlational laws' are not 'natural laws' and cannot fulfil the requirements of measurement that are accepted in science. Consequently he thinks that neurophenomenological laws cannot be used to make sense of the causal relationships between consciousness and brain.

In assessing how **Rakover**'s commentary relates to my TA it is important to first note that he does not actually *address* the detailed account that I have given of how to make sense of the causal relationships of consciousness and brain, nor of the way that potential neurophenomenological laws might fit into such an account. However he does offer a critique of the scientific status of neurophenomenological laws as such, and of the use of 'information' as a unit of measurement in psychology. As these are important elements of my analysis I will confine my reply to these relevant aspects of his critique. Second, although **Rakover** gives the misleading impression at the beginning of his commentary that my use of neurophenomenological laws is out of step with psychological practice in that it does not conform to 'rules of the game that are accepted by the natural sciences and cognitive psychology' (p. 53 above), he goes on to admit at the end of his commentary that my use of such correlational relationships is entirely conventional within psychology and that his real target is psychology! As he concludes on page 57, his critique 'could also be directed at psychology at large. In comparison with research in the natural sciences, psychological research is limited and does not progress like physics (see Rakover, 1992)'.

What are these supposed limitations on psychological research? According to **Rakover**, neurophenomenological laws do not fulfil the requirement for the 'unit equivalency' found in natural laws such as Newton's law of gravity, where the units of measurement found on both sides of the equation $S = 1/2GT^2$ can be shown to be equivalent. Let us suppose, for example, that neuropsychology discovers the exact neural correlates of different subjective aspects of pain phenomenology and manages to express its findings in neurophenomenological laws. In such cases, **Rakover** asks, 'Can it be shown that the combination of the units of measurement on the right-hand side of the pain equation is identical to the combination of the units on the left-hand side? To the best of my knowledge the answer is no' (p. 53). I agree. But such an absence of unit equivalency provides yet another argument against *reductive physicalism*. It has nothing to do with whether or not there *are* distinct physical/functional correlates of distinct pain experiences, or with whether or not it is possible to chart such relationships precisely in the form of *nonreductive* neurophenomenological laws that do not require 'unit equivalency'.

But would the absence of 'unit equivalency' make neurophenomenological laws unscientific? Consider **Rakover**'s doubts about studies of pain phenomenology. Pain is often presented as a paradigm case of a private, subjective, mental event within philosophy of mind. There are many ways to measure the subjective experience of pain,[10] but at the present time no valid 'objective' measure of pain experience (in terms of a physiological index) exists. In spite of this, over the period 1960 to 2002, the Medline database lists around 200,000 publications on pain and its alleviation, making it a heavily investigated area of medicine. According to Rakover, such studies are restricted by the absence of 'fundamental measurement units' of the kind that obtain, say, for the measurement of length, which sustain properties such as transitivity and additivity. While this is true, it is hardly news to anyone trained in psychological research, where it is taken for granted that whenever numbers are assigned to psychological variables these must be scaled in a way that is appropriate to those variables (reaction time and error rate merit a ratio scale, subjective judgements of magnitude generally merit an ordinal scale, categorical judgements a nominal scale, and so on). Once an appropriate scale is assigned, numbers derived from measurements of behaviour or subjective judgements can be subjected to appropriate statistical analyses, and the results interpreted as supporting hypotheses (or not) in the normal way.[11]

It is true that few relationships between physical and psychological variables have been found to be sufficiently general and orderly to merit the term 'law' and even these do not satisfy 'unit equivalency.' Perhaps the best example is Stevens' power law $J = kI^x$ where J is the judged intensity of a stimulus (e.g. its brightness or loudness), k is a scaling constant, I is the physical intensity (e.g. specified in lumens or decibels), and x is a constant whose value depends on the modality of the judged stimulus (e.g. for judged loudness, x = 0.3). Stevens' law charts how variations in the physical stimuli are translated into judged changes in the way those stimuli are experienced. Consequently it is 'correlational' in precisely the

---

[10] Standard measuring instruments include verbal rating scales, numerical rating scales, visual analogue scales and questionnaires such as the McGill Pain Questionnaire (Melzack, 1987).

[11] **Rakover** also complains that phenomenal measurements cannot meet the requirements of objectivity, publicity, and repeatability. I disagree. However this is a large topic on which I have written on extensively, both in this journal (Velmans, 1999) and in *Understanding Consciousness*, chapter 8. Given the limitations on space in this reply I ask interested readers to refer to these prior sources.

way that **Rakover** describes. Does this mean that Stevens' law is unscientific? No. There are countless examples in science where Nature does not fit into the neat conceptual boxes that we have prepared for her, and the psychological and biological sciences have long abandoned the view that the only relationships of scientific interest are fundamental causal laws of the kind found in physics. Functional models in cognitive psychology and compositional accounts of the structure of biological systems are obvious cases in point. In psychophysics, Stevens' power law may not satisfy unit equivalency, but it nevertheless expresses empirically verifiable relationships between physical dimensions of stimuli and subjective judgements about those stimuli in a precise, systematic way, and it is in that sense unquestionably scientific. Given this, it is reasonable to hope that in some future neuroscience it may be possible to develop neurophenomenological laws with equivalent precision and generality.

   Rakover also claims that information cannot be a unit of psychological measurement. But again, few psychologists would agree. It is true that, following George Miller's (1956) seminal paper 'The magical number 7 ± 2', psychologists have long accepted that human mental processing is often too flexible and varied to be computable in 'bits' in the precise Shannon sense. Nonetheless the psychological use of concepts derived from information theory and/or the more general principles of information processing developed within electrical engineering is ubiquitous — to the point that, in cognitive psychology, mental processing is habitually referred to as human information processing. In any case, my own use of the terms 'information' and 'information structure' relate to a fairly precise use of these terms that is applicable in psychophysics, for example in the study of difference limens (minimal discriminable differences). Such studies document whether or not physically measurable differences in stimuli are translated or not (by sensory/perceptual processes) into consciously perceived differences, that is whether or not information about physical differences is translated into detectable changes in phenomenology.[12] In the same way it is possible to study whether or not physical/functional differences in neural representations of stimuli are translated into detectable changes in phenomenology. Physical/functional changes in neural representational states that are translated may be said to be of the same 'grain' as the conscious phenomenology and to mirror its information structure. **Rakover** doubts that it would be possible to identify such information bearing states, as one cannot remove one's dependence on subjective reports of what is or is not experienced. I agree that one cannot remove subjective reports. However, the combination of subjective reports with triangulating third-person observations of neural states is standard practice in neuropsychology. Investigation of the neural correlates of consciousness is technically difficult, but the field

---

[12] If the physical differences can be consciously perceived we can say that information about physically measurable differences has been successfully 'transmitted' or transformed into discriminable, phenomenal differences. Note that it is often possible for physical differences in stimuli to be detected in spite of not being consciously perceived (for example if subjects are required to guess). As this is tangential to the point at issue I will not elaborate on it here.

of investigation is already very large (cf Metzinger, 2000). Rather than being questionable science, it is unquestionably normal science.

Analogies

The ways in which different conscious experiences relate to their physical correlates have to be understood in their own terms. Some properties of these relationships appear to resemble ones that are already well understood in natural science, but, as far as one can tell, no other purely physical system provides an exact homology. Crucially, the relations of experiences to their physical correlates have to be understood in terms of how certain phenomena (the experiences) viewed from a first-person perspective relate to other phenomena (the correlated brain states) viewed from a third-person perspective. By contrast, *all* the properties of physical systems (conventionally understood) can be viewed from a third-person perspective.

Videotapes and TV screens. Sometimes, however, analogies can help. For example, to understand how experiences and their physical correlates might encode identical information without themselves being identical it is useful to know that such a dissociation between representations and representing systems are commonplace in technology — as in my example of the play 'Hamlet' encoded on videotape or displayed on a screen. Given my limited intent, it is hard to understand **Chrisley & Sloman**'s claim that this analogy 'misfires'. As they correctly note, 'this is not an ontological reduction'. However, according to them, 'it is an epistemological one', and then they go on to claim that, 'epistemological dualism is the only thing separating Velmans from the physicalist positions he rejects'. But how can this be?

Videotapes and TV screens encode information in entirely different formats. Even when they encode information about the same thing, they do so in two entirely different ways — which is broadly analogous to knowing about one thing in two different ways. So in what sense is this an 'epistemological reduction'? Admittedly, there is one known, the nature of mind, with two (material and phenomenal) aspects, by which it can be known. But, given that I suggest the nature of mind to be 'psychophysical', in what sense is this 'physicalist'?[13]

---

[13] **Chrisley & Sloman** go on to claim, 'It is this need to distance himself from physicalism which raises the second problem with the analogy: he admits that the videotape and the screen are ontologically distinct, yet he was supposedly defending an 'ontologically monist' position! It seems Velmans ends up with the converse of the position for which he was aiming: ontological dualism, but epistemological monism (in the sense that strong assumptions are made about 'informational mirroring').' This confused analysis of the intent of my videotape/TV screen analogy needs some unravelling. It is true that conscious experiences and their neural correlates have distinct (phenomenal and physical) characteristics and in that sense may be said to have distinct ontologies. But this does not prevent them being aspects of an underlying, unified mind, thereby making my dual-aspect theory ontologically monist (in the tradition of Spinoza). Nor does the possession of distinct phenomenal and physical characteristics prevent experiences and their correlates from encoding identical information. The videotape/TV screen analogy provides one example of how representational systems can encode identical information without having identical characteristics. It should have been obvious that I did not mean to suggest that brain states are *literally* a form of videotape and experiences *literally* a kind of TV screen or that experiences can somehow be *decoupled* from their physical correlates! Nor does it make sense to interpret the view that one can know (or represent) one thing in *two different ways* 'epistemological monism.'

Electricity and magnetism. The same information can be formatted differently, depending on the characteristics of the representing system. If one can specify the different ways that given information is formatted, then it should be possible, in principle, to specify how those different formats map onto each other. In TA and Velmans (2000) I suggest that, in some future neuropsychology it might be possible to specify how the phenomenology of given conscious experiences map onto to their physical correlates in this way. This might provide a dual- aspect account of the nature of mind in which the relationships between its physical and phenomenal aspects were specified precisely, perhaps with the precision that electrical current in a wire can be related to its surrounding magnetic field.[14]

Chrisley & Sloman confusingly suggests that the duality that I have in mind with the electromagnetism analogy, 'is one of aspects, not of ontological character.' What I actually suggest is that the phenomenal and physical aspects of mind *specify* its (psychophysical) ontological character.[15] Even more confusingly they go on to write, '... the analogy doesn't work: electricity and magnetism are not simply two ways of thinking about the same phenomenon, but two different physical phenomena that can be related to each other mathematically.' Given that I never suggest that electricity and magnetism are simply two ways of thinking about electromagnetism (rather than genuine aspects), nor that physical and phenomenal aspects of mind are simply two ways of thinking about mind (rather than genuine aspects) the relevance of this comment to my analysis is hard to understand. They then add to the confusion by going on to write, 'In contrast, and crucially, Velmans claims that the difference between first and third person ways of thinking of psychophysical stuff is merely that of differently formatted ways of representing the same information.' I claim nothing of the sort. As noted above, first- and third-person (phenomenal and physical) aspects of mind are not merely different 'ways of thinking' about it. Being genuine phenomenal and physical *aspects* (or manifestations) of mind, they can in principle encode the same information in different phenomenal and physical formats. **Chrisley & Sloman** go on to note that 'the electrical phenomenon is not just an aspect, a way of formatting the same information as that represented by the magnetic way of looking at the situation. There are situations where only the electrical description applies, and other situations where only the magnetic description applies.' I agree — although this again has nothing to do with my analysis of dual-aspect monism or my use of the electricity/magnetism analogy.[16] They go on

---

[14] As it happens, a psychophysical theory relating information encoded in the brain's electrochemistry to a pooled, integrated form of the same information encoded in the brain's electromagnetic field has recently been proposed in this journal by McFadden (2002a,b). According to McFadden this EM field is the physical substrate of phenomenal consciousness (see also Pockett, 2002; John, 2002). While I am not committed to the details of this theory, and do not think it solves the 'hard' problem (the EM field would still have to have dual-aspects to bridge the gap from physics to phenomenal experience), it does illustrate the type of theory that I have in mind.

[15] The fact that one has different (first- and third-person) forms of access to these (phenomenal and physical) aspects of mind does not alter the point that these aspects specify the mind's ontology.

[16] It is hard to know what **Chrisley & Sloman** mean by a 'magnetic way of looking at the situation.' Unlike them, I do not confound the dual-aspect ontology of mind, or the way information is formatted within its phenomenal and physical aspects, with first- versus third-person ways of examining the

to conclude that, 'Prima facie, this suggests that there are two distinct phenomena involved; to argue that there is actually only one, root phenomenon will require further work from Velmans.' Here I disagree. Electricity and magnetism are indeed distinct phenomena, but the view that they are both manifestations of only one root phenomenon (electromagnetism) is received wisdom in physics. It requires no further work from me.[17]

Wave–particle complementarity. In TA note 13 and in Velmans (2000) I note that my dual-aspect analysis of mind also has some interesting resemblances to wave–particle complementarity in quantum mechanics — although, once again, the analogy is far from exact. Quanta either appear to behave as electromagnetic waves or as particles depending on the observation arrangements. And it does not make sense to claim that electromagnetic waves really are particles (or vice versa). A complete understanding of quanta requires both complementary descriptions. First- and third-person observations of mind also depend on very different observational arrangements, so that may help to explain why, from a first-person perspective it takes the form of conscious phenomenology, whereas viewed from the outside it appears to be a brain. Like wave-particle accounts in quantum mechanics, phenomenal and physical accounts of the mind's operations appear to be complementary and mutually irreducible. A complete account of mind requires both.

Note that these distinguishing features of dual-aspect monism contrast sharply with competing analyses of the experience/brain state relationship. Substance dualists maintain that experiences and correlated brain states are entirely different 'substances' or 'entities', idealists argue that all physical entities (including brain states) are really forms of mind or consciousness (**Rao**), and physicalists argue that experiences are nothing more than states of the brain (**Torrance**, **Van Gulick**, **Chrisley & Sloman**). All these positions have well known problems. For example, dualism splits the universe in a way that makes it difficult to get it together again, idealism does not cope well with the apparent, autonomous existence of the material world, and physicalism does not cope well with the phenomenology of conscious experience. I have argued that dual-aspect monism allows one to accommodate first- and third-person evidence in a more natural way that avoids such problems. While the case for this above (and in Velmans, 1991; 2000; and TA) does not rely in any way on analogies from other branches of science, the parallel with wave-particle complementarity in quantum mechanics is suggestive.

---

mind's phenomenal and physical aspects. Likewise, I do not confound the electrical and magnetic manifestations of electromagnetism, or the possibility of encoding information in either electrical or magnetic formats, with the different ways in which we can investigate electricity and magnetism.

[17] As I point out in TA note 14, I am only concerned here with the broader implications of dual-aspect monism. Consequently, it seems to me useful to suggest that there might be a psychophysical unity underlying the phenomenal and physical aspects of mind, that is broadly analogous to the electromagnetic unity underlying electricity and magnetism. It goes without saying that I am not suggesting that conscious phenomenology *is* magnetism, or that its physical correlates *are* electricity. The precise way that given conscious experiences map onto their physical correlates can only be discovered by neuropsychological research and, in this sense, 'requires further work'.

However, according to **Chrisley & Sloman**, this analogy 'is even worse' — although they take issue not with me, but with the founders of quantum mechanics. They write,

> More and more physicists and philosophers take the appeal to complementarity as a *reductio ad absurdum* of particular ontological positions in quantum mechanics. They do not deny the veracity of the data that have led some to conclude that quanta have both wave and particle aspects; but they do deny that the paradox of complementarity is a satisfying way of accounting for that data. There are other, less paradoxical and thus more satisfying metaphysical pictures on offer (e.g. Bohm, 1952; Hiley and Pylkkänen, 2001). To say that your metaphysics of mind is akin to the wave/particle complementarity metaphysics of quanta is just another way of saying that you don't have a satisfying metaphysics, and choose instead to 'live with' the paradoxes (p. 62 above).

I think that is being rather unfair to our colleagues in physics. The majority of physicists are more concerned with whether the mathematics of QM accounts for the data, and they think of (exclusive) complementarity as a current, best description of the empirical findings, imposed by the limitations of measurement, rather than 'a *reductio ad absurdum* of particular ontological positions'. Nor is there any emerging consensus about what would be a satisfying metaphysics. As it happens, I share **Chrisley & Sloman**'s interest in more classical accounts of QM findings (in spite of this being a minority view in physics). According to Bohm and his collaborators, wave-like and particle-like behaviour are manifestations of a unified, grounding reality (Bohm often refers to this as an 'implicate order') just as I have claimed experiences and their physical correlates to be dual-aspects of a unified, psychophysical mind. So adopting a classical metaphysics in QM (in the way that **Chrisley & Sloman** suggest) would make the analogy with dual-aspect monism even closer!

In sum, let me stress again that analogies have their purposes, but they are not homologies. The analogies that I have used illustrate how phenomenal and physical representational systems might format the same information in different ways, and how phenomenal and physical aspects of mind might be tightly bound to each other without reducing to each other. But I do not claim consciousness to be literally a picture on a TV screen, a magnetic field, or a wave-like QM phenomenon (to claim all three simultaneously would in any case be absurd). The relation of any given conscious experience to its physical correlates has to be understood in its own terms.

A Re-Examination of What We Take For Granted

What has ontological primacy — consciousness or the physical world? In current Western philosophy and science the existence of the physical world is generally taken for granted, while the existence of consciousness is thought to be somewhat mysterious. The physical world is also generally assumed to be the primary reality on which other 'emergent' forms of existence such as mind and consciousness depend. **Chrisley & Sloman** for example, take it for granted that the physical/experiential relationship is asymmetrical. Physical states can exist without accompanying experiences (e.g. in the form of preconscious brain states) — but conscious experiences cannot exist without accompanying physical states. As they note, 'The only way to impose symmetry would be to assume (as others have been forced to do, e.g. Chalmers, 1996) that whenever there is a physical phenomenon, there is some experiential phenomenon, however slight or imperceptible or implausible, accompanying it. Panpsychism threatens.'

It is instructive to note however that such opinions about what has ontological primacy and what constitutes a 'threat' (to right thinking) are not universal. As **Rao** points out, very different views about the ontological status and distribution of consciousness and mind dominate in philosophical traditions that have developed in the East. In these traditions, the irreducibility of consciousness to brain states is taken for granted and consciousness, not the physical world, is thought to be primary. In some Indian traditions for example, the physical world is thought to be a projection of consciousness constructed by the mind.

How is it possible that thinkers in the West and the East have come to such very different conclusions? Note that the ontological primacy of either consciousness or the physical world is not obvious from the immediate, empirical 'evidence of our senses' for the simple reason that, in everyday life, conscious experience and what we normally think of as the 'physical world' *co-arise*. That is to say, what we normally think of as the physical world just *is* the 3D phenomenal world that we experience.[18] However, Western and Eastern thinkers have traditionally taken a very different *interest* in what is experienced. Western 'third-person' science has traditionally been interested in experience as a means to an end, namely the nature, control and transformation of the entities and events that such experiences *represent* (what they are experiences *of*) and has developed investigative methods and technologies appropriate to these interests. By contrast, Eastern 'first-person' philosophy and science has traditionally been interested in the nature, control and transformation of the experiences *themselves*, and has developed methods appropriate to these aims. I suggest that these different foci of interest and accompanying methodologies partly explain East–West differences of opinion about what has ontological primacy.

It is not altogether surprising that if one's third-person investigative attention is entirely focused on the material entities and events that one's experiences represent, one might conclude their fundamental nature to be entirely material. Many external entities and events appear to exist whether they are experienced or not, thereby supporting their ontological primacy and a form of physical realism. In the human brain some processes appear to be accompanied by consciousness while others appear to be preconscious, unconscious or nonconscious, suggesting a physical/experience asymmetry. Viewed from the outside, the material forms of entities and events are evident, but not any accompanying experience,

---

[18] The appearance of the 3D phenomenal physical world is not of course identical to the more abstract world described by physics (quantum mechanics, relativity, string theory and so on). The relation of the phenomenal physical world to the world described by physics is central to a proper understanding of the consciousness/material world relationship and I discuss this in depth in *Understanding Consciousness*, chapters 6 and 7. As this relationship is somewhat tangential to the issues raised in TA and the commentaries I will not elaborate on it here.

even in other human beings (the problem of 'other minds'). Consequently pan-psychism looks dubious.

On the other hand, if one's first-person investigative attention is focused in ever finer ways on conscious experience itself it is not surprising that one might conclude its fundamental nature to be a refined form of consciousness (tradition-ally a 'pure', contentless consciousness). Conscious experience is in any case 'immediately given' and is epistemically primary in the sense that it provides the foundation for the acquisition of all empirical knowledge. Indeed, what we nor-mally think of as the 'physical world' just is the 3D *phenomenal* world that forms part of everyday conscious experience (see above). Conversely, without con-scious experience this *phenomenal* physical world would not exist (a form of ide-alism), thereby providing grounds for the Eastern view that consciousness has ontological primacy.

Which view is correct? It is not possible to attempt a full analysis in a few lines. However, in *Understanding Consciousness* and TA I develop a dual-aspect, reflexive monism that treads a careful path between taking either a first- or third-person approach to be more privileged or fundamental. Rather, these perspectives are complementary and mutually irreducible. For example, in Velmans (1990b; 2000, ch. 7) I suggest that Eastern idealism and Western real-ism may both be true although they are true about different things. Idealism may be said to apply to the observer-dependent existence of the *phenomenal* world while realism applies to the observer-independent existence of the entities and events (things themselves) that experienced phenomena *represent*. Under normal conditions, *neither* a first- nor a third-person perspective provides a 'view from nowhere,' that is a view of the thing-itself as it is in-itself, even if the aspect of the thing-itself under scrutiny is the human mind. Conversely, both investigative routes can lead to deeper knowledge. Third-person science provides a deeper knowledge of the material world, understood in a third-person way. First-person investigations of consciousness provide a deeper knowledge of one's own mind, understood in a first-person way. My route to this position is an entirely conven-tional Western one, relying on the normal triangulation of scientific evidence, everyday experience, common sense and theory. Nevertheless, once the implica-tions of this position are fully worked out (in terms of what consciousness is and does, and how it relates to the brain and the physical world) the *Reflexive Monism* that results takes one a long way from current Western materialism. I conclude for example that

> Human minds, bodies and brains are embedded in a far greater universe. Individual conscious representations are perspectival. That is, the precise manner in which entities, events and processes are translated into experiences depends on the loca-tion in space and time of a given observer, and the exact mix of perceptual, cogni-tive, affective, social, cultural and historical influences which enter into the 'construction' of a given experience. In this sense, each conscious construction is private, subjective, and unique. Taken together, the contents of consciousness pro-vide a view of the wider universe, giving it the appearance of a 3D phenomenal world. This results from a reflexive interaction of entities, events and processes

with our perceptual and cognitive systems that, in turn, represent those entities, events and processes. However, conscious representations are not the thing-itself. In this vision, there is one universe (the thing-itself), with relatively differentiated parts in the form of conscious beings like ourselves, each with a unique, conscious view of the larger universe of which it is a part. In so far as we are parts of the universe that, in turn, experience the larger universe, we participate in a reflexive process whereby the universe experiences itself (Velmans, 2000, p. 233).

Later, I add, 'In this sense, we participate in a process whereby the universe observes itself — and the universe becomes both the subject and object of experience. Consciousness and matter are intertwined in mind. Through the evolution of matter, consciousness is given *form*. And through consciousness, the material universe is *real-ized*' (p. 280). It is not possible to summarize the full implications of reflexive monism in a few lines, let alone the case supporting it. However, as **Rao** notes, my route appears to travel from West to East. His only complaint is that I have not traveled far enough! While I do not have space to deal with how *Understanding Consciousness* relates to various Eastern philosophies in any detail, Rao's comments provide a welcome opportunity to assess the internal coherence of TA (and *Understanding Consciousness*) from a very different perspective, and it is instructive to address his main points.[19]

From West to East?

Any comparison of Eastern and Western views of 'consciousness' and 'mind' has to start with a clarification of terms, for the simple reason that in the West and the East the terms 'consciousness' and 'mind' are habitually used in different ways. As **Rao** notes, I largely confine my use of the term 'consciousness' to *phenomenal consciousness* — the everyday experience of the external world, the body, and inner experiences (such as thoughts, feelings and so on). Although there are many uses of the term 'consciousness' in the West, phenomenal consciousness is arguably closest to its most common usage. Crucially, it is consciousness in the sense of 'phenomenal consciousness' that poses 'hard' problems of the kind currently discussed in Western philosophy such as 'How could conscious experiences affect the activity of brains?' (the subject of TA). I also largely follow current Western conventions in my use of the term 'mind.' As with 'consciousness' the term mind has various uses. However, in psychology it is typical to think of the human mind as that which enables us to *function* in certain ways (to think, to solve problems and so on). Although the details of how consciousness, mind and brain relate are in dispute, there is consensus that 'mind' is intimately connected to both brain and consciousness. A major finding of twentieth century psychology is that mental processes may or may not 'be conscious.' Some processes have associated phenomenal contents, while others are

---

[19] **Rao** also raises a number of questions in passing, for example, what is meant by 'information structure', what encodes that information, how does 'perspectival switching' work, and in what sense is information viewed from a first- and a third-person perspective complementary. As I have dealt with these issues earlier in this reply I won't return to them here.

preconscious, unconscious, or nonconscious. Consequently, in Western psychology, 'mind' is commonly thought of as *encompassing* consciousness.

Eastern common usage of the terms 'consciousness' and 'mind' is somewhat different. However it is not difficult to tease out terminological differences from genuine, theoretical ones. At first glance, the Samkhya-Yoga tradition described by **Rao** might look very different to Reflexive Monism. In this tradition, consciousness, with *purusha* [20] at its centre, forms the ground of one's individual being. It is the contentless container within which perspectival, phenomenal consciousness takes form. Mind, unlike consciousness, is physical in that it can be described in material forms and accounted for in physical terms.

> The *purusha* as the centre of consciousness is distinct and has unique experiences through its associated mind-body complex. Such observer dependent relativity, in Yoga as well as in Vedanta, is not absolutely given but a transient condition that can be overcome by disciplined practice. The *purusha* finds itself reflected in the mind illuminating the material forms of the universe. Thus mind becomes as instrument through which the universe reveals itself. Subject-object distinction is not fundamental. It is a contingent manifestation of the mental process by which the universe is revealed (p. 65).

In my own analysis in *Understanding Consciousness* I am careful to remain within the evidence base currently accepted by Western science, and I tease the modern problems of consciousness away from more traditional concerns with the nature of the 'soul' (Velmans, 2000, pp. 15–16). Consequently, I do not comment on the existence or operations of 'purusha'. While I have no doubt that first-person investigative attention can lead to a deeper understanding of mind (see above) I also remain neutral about whether disciplined practice can *entirely* remove one's observer dependent relativity, or whether the ensuing conscious state can be *entirely* contentless (Velmans, 2000, ch. 1, note 2).[21] Nevertheless,

---

[20] In the Samkhya-Yoga tradition, Purusha refers to one's true, individual, immaterial essence (also referred to as Atman or soul).

[21] **Rao** writes that 'Velmans speaks of direct and indirect knowledge, as the Indian theories do. ... In Yoga theory, even the so-called first-person experience is indirect, because what the mind presents to consciousness are representations mediated by the perceptual and cognitive systems. Consequently, awareness arising from such mediation is also indirect. In other words, in Velmans, the direct acquaintance is with the representations, whereas in Yoga it is with the things themselves. Such direct knowledge results when the mind detaches itself from the sensory inputs and makes contact directly with the objects, events and processes in the universe. This is what may be labelled as paranormal process distinguished from the normal process in which there is the involvement of the sensory processes' (pp. 67–8). However, this doesn't quite capture the similarities and differences between Reflexive Monism and the Yoga theory that Rao describes. In Velmans, 2000, ch. 7, I develop the view that, under normal conditions, we have direct acquaintance with our own experiences but only indirect acquaintance with the things-themselves that such experiences represent. Given that normal experiences are representations, I agree with the Yoga view that they only provide indirect knowledge of things themselves, even when the things themselves that we experience are the operations of our own minds. Nevertheless, *contra* Kant, I argue that the thing-itself (including mind-itself) is knowable through the representations that we have of it, and the aim of both first- and third-person science is to achieve deeper, more complete knowledge. Knowledge can be gained through direct acquaintance, by experiencing that which one seeks to know, or indirectly, through the use of symbols (description, theory and so on). But it is only through direct experience that things become *subjectively real* for us (we *real-ize* what they are like). One can only really know love for example by real-izing what it is like to be in love. This, I think, gets quite close to the Yoga view, with the caution that I remain non committal about the possibility (often suggested in Yoga philosophy) that it is possible for embodied human beings to *fully* know (real-ize) the thing-

there are broad similarities between Reflexive Monism and the Eastern view that Rao describes. Like Samkya-Yoga philosophy (and Western materialism) I accept that mind has (third-person) physical *aspects* that provide an instrument for the formation of phenomenal consciousness. I also accept that both phenomenal consciousness and material aspects of mind are grounded in something deeper, namely a self-revealing universe in which the subject-object distinction is not fundamental (see above). However, in my own analysis the terms I use to refer to what is deeper are different. For example, 'consciousness with *purusha* at its center', is replaced by the 'deeper nature of mind' (or, in Kantian fashion, 'mind-itself').[22]

These different uses of terms partly account for a number of confusions in **Rao**'s summary of my own theoretical position. **Rao** notes that both Indian theories and my own make a distinction between consciousness and mind. But he suggests that, 'In the Indian view; the distinction is fundamental and primary in the sense that one is not reducible to the other. In Velmans' view, the distinction is secondary and holds good at the epistemological level and not at the ontological level. Thus consciousness becomes a subcategory or species of the mind.'

In fact, however, I never suggest that 'consciousness' *interpreted in the broad Eastern sense* is an aspect of the material mind *interpreted in the narrow Eastern sense* (that would indeed be inconsistent with my view that consciousness cannot be reduced to states of the brain). What I actually suggest is that *phenomenal* consciousness (understood in the conventional Western sense) is an aspect of the deeper nature of mind (mind-itself). The neural correlates of consciousness and other forms of brain functioning provide the complementary, material aspect of mind-itself. Being genuine aspects, both consciousness and brain have an *ontology*, as well as providing first- and third-person means by which the mind can be known. Consequently **Rao** is wrong to suggest that the distinction between mind and consciousness in my own work is purely epistemological. And he mistakes my suggestion that mind-itself encompasses consciousness to mean that the *material aspect* of mind encompasses consciousness. Rather, the deeper, psychophysical nature of mind encompasses both its manifest conscious and material aspects.[23]

If one replaces **Rao**'s Eastern use of the term 'consciousness' with my use of the term 'mind-itself' or more broadly 'the thing-itself' one immediately clears up a number of other confusions. Rao writes for example, 'the distinction between first-person consciousness and third-person consciousness adds little to the clarity of the concept of consciousness. Consciousness is consciousness whether we look at it from a first-person or the third-person perspective. It may manifest different characteristics at different levels of observation, but it underlies all awareness. Consciousness is what makes awareness possible. It is the

---

itself as it is in itself, that is to have 'direct' knowledge in the sense of knowledge that is 'perfect and complete'. Nor do I comment in Velmans (2000) on the nature and existence of paranormal phenomena.

[22] In this usage, mind-itself is that aspect of the thing-itself (the ground of being) that forms the basis of the manifest aspects of one's own mind (i.e. its third-person, material and first-person, phenomenal consciousness aspects).

ground condition for all forms of awareness, like matter which is the ground condition for all the material forms we experience' (p. 66 above).

Viewed in conventional Western terms, **Rao**'s statement makes no sense, for the reason that phenomenal consciousness cannot be viewed from a third-person perspective (whatever the level of observation). In the West, the terms consciousness, phenomenal consciousness and conscious awareness are often used interchangeably (I do so in my own work). Consequently it makes no sense to suggest that consciousness underlies awareness (it cannot underlie itself). The suggestion that 'consciousness is the ground condition for all forms of awareness, like matter which is the ground condition for all the material forms we experience' is also inconsistent with the view that consciousness has ontological primacy *over* matter (the alternative is ontological dualism). By contrast, 'mind-itself' *can* be viewed from first- and third-person perspectives, *does* underlie phenomenal consciousness and is the ground condition for both its conscious and material manifestations (thereby avoiding dualism).

Of course, these different terms for what has ontological primacy in the East and in the West (and their corresponding descriptions) also reflect substantive theoretical differences. In Samkya-Yoga philosophy 'consciousness with *purusha* at its center' is the fundamental reality. In Western materialism the physical world is the fundamental reality. In **Rao**'s opinion I have to choose between these: if I reject the reducibility of conscious experience to brain states, I must accept the primacy of consciousness. Not so. I accept that if one investigates the mind from a third-person Western perspective it will appear to be entirely physical while if one investigates it from a first-person Eastern perspective it will appear to be entirely conscious experience (see above). But, as far as I can judge, neither route to knowledge of the mind is privileged, incorrigible or complete. Rather, first- and third-person routes to knowledge of the mind are complementary and mutually irreducible. Consequently, the 'deeper nature of mind' (mind-itself) is better described as psychophysical.

Rao suggests that, in my own analysis, there is an asymmetry between conscious states which do not reduce to states of the brain and nonconscious mental activities which do reduce to brain states. In his view this leads to 'the real problem.' He writes, 'Velmans acknowledges that consciousness is not reducible to brain states or functions. Yet, he considers consciousness an aspect of the mind.

---

[23] Other confusions in Rao's commentary can be traced to differences in use of terms combined with differences that arise from taking a first-person route to the nature of mind to be more primary than a third-person route. Rao for example claims that equating consciousness with phenomenal consciousness entails confusion 'between the contents and the container, between substance and form.' I accept that, viewed from an Eastern first-person perspective, a form of pure contentless consciousness might appear to underlie everyday phenomenal consciousness, and the former therefore is viewed as the container of the latter. However, my own, somewhat different dual-aspect analysis does not confuse contents and container, or substance and form. Rather, the container is mind-itself and the suggested nature of this container is a little different. While I remain open to the view that with appropriate first-person training, the nature of mind itself appears as a form of pure, contentless consciousness, dual-aspect monism would suggest that even a conscious state as basic as this would have correspondingly basic, physical aspects that could, in principle, be discovered by empirical research. As the nature of mind-itself encompasses all its aspects it seems more accurate to describe it as psychophysical.

The mind in his view is broader to include nonconscious mental activities as well. Here rests the real problem. Consciousness (subjective experience) is irreducible to neural states or brain functions, whereas the nonsubjective states of the mind are in principle reducible. In the light of such a fundamental difference between them, it is hardly plausible to argue that consciousness is a species or an aspect of the mind. The irreducibility of consciousness to physical states entails that the difference between conscious and nonconscious aspects of the mind is one of kind, primary and fundamental. Reducibility or otherwise of one category into another is an ontological matter and not simply an epistemological issue' (p. 66).

Epistemological symmetries and asymmetries between first- and third-person perspectives are important, but I agree with **Rao** that reducibility is an ontological matter, not an epistemological matter. However, such an ontological asymmetry between conscious states and nonconscious ones would occur only if the nonconscious nature of mind turned out to be entirely physical (as **Rao** himself assumes). If so, conscious mind would have dual-aspects, but nonconscious mind would only have a physical aspect. As it happens, a similar view to this is held by those 'nonreductive physicalists' that adopt property dualism. Whether this leads to a 'real problem' depends on whether such asymmetries actually occur in nature or not (if they do, it would be perverse to regard them as a problem). **Chrisley & Sloman** for example take such asymmetries for granted. As they note, 'There is a fundamental asymmetry between the physical and the conscious: Physical laws apply everywhere, both in situations where there is and where there is not consciousness, while the converse does not hold. So there seems to be a primacy of the physical, and one must reply to the idea that it is this physical, causal reality which is always doing all the work' (p. 59). **Rao** adopts the opposite view that a pure consciousness without any material form is the basis of everything, but does not appear to recognize that this produces an inverse asymmetry (in which physical matter becomes secondary to consciousness).

Whether such asymmetries actually occur in Nature is up to Nature — and whether they do or not is largely tangential to the analysis of consciousness that I have given in TA and in Velmans (2000). It is important to note however that, unlike both materialism and idealism, ontological asymmetries are avoidable in dual-aspect theory, which allows for the possibility that mind-itself has a dual-aspect, psychophysical nature *irrespective of whether its operations are unconscious, preconscious or conscious*. [24] On this interpretation, the dual-aspect

[24] My analysis of consciousness (in TA and in *Understanding Consciousness*, chapters 1–11) deals largely with phenomenal consciousness in humans and is consequently neutral about whether there is a first-person aspect (latent or manifest) in states other than those that actually have manifestations in (recognisable) conscious experience. *Understanding Consciousness*, chapter 12, however, is more speculative and considers the evolution and distribution of consciousness. It compares 'discontinuity' theory (that consciousness appeared suddenly at a given point in evolution) with 'continuity' theory (that the potential for recognisable consciousness was there from the beginning and evolved in form as matter evolved in form). Although little of my detailed analysis of consciousness depends on it, I argue that the latter is more intellectually elegant, and it fits more naturally into Reflexive Monism. The view that consciousness is a natural accompaniment of material forms also has implications for how one might think about the necessary and sufficient conditions for consciousness in the human

nature of mind is fully manifest only in those aspects of mind that are 'conscious'. However, with appropriate investigative techniques, some preconscious and unconscious aspects of the mind can *become* conscious (in the sense that we can become aware of those aspects or to real-ize their nature).[25] Unconscious and preconscious aspects of mind can also be thought of as psychophysical in the sense that they can have *causal effects* on both conscious experiences and physical states of the body/brain, for example in the operation of preconscious free will (see TA).[26]

Note that *whatever* view one adopts about what is primary, one is left with the problem of origins. In the West, we generally accept that the origins and existence of consciousness are somewhat mysterious (when and why did it emerge?). But we habitually ignore the fact that the origins and existence of matter are equally mysterious. Why should there be anything rather than nothing? As the origins of a 'psychophysical mind' are also mysterious, the choice between these three positions has to be made on other grounds.

Which view is preferable? Note that there are 'hard' problems associated with taking either the material world or conscious experience to be more primary than the other. In the West it is well recognized that taking the material world to be primary leaves one with the problem of consciousness. How could something like an experience emerge from a material world that does not already have it? It is perhaps less well recognized in the East that if one takes the existence of consciousness to be primary one is left with the inverse problem. How could something like an independently existing material world emerge from something like an experience? If the thing-itself and mind-itself are *fundamentally* psychophysical one avoids such problems.[27] And one can then make sense of mind/body interactions observed in clinical practice and everyday life.

---

brain. Rather than thinking of consciousness as something that is mysteriously *added* to representations at the focus of attention, it can be thought of a natural aspect of neural information processing as such. Why is it apparently absent in unconscious and preconscious processing? One possibility is that, in the evolution of complex brains with multiple sources of information, massive inhibition of information became a biological necessity to enable focus on information of greatest importance, and with it, inhibition of consciousness. On this view, unconscious and preconscious mental processes have inhibited consciousness. Conversely, information at the focus of attention is subject to release from inhibition (see Arbuthnott, 1995, for a review of the evidence, and the discussion of this and alternative theories in Velmans, 1995). Another possibility is that representations at the focus of attention are activated to a degree that masks any consciousness associated with other representations, rather like an orchestra on stage masks whispers in the audience.

[25] Many methods have been developed in both the West and the East for gaining conscious access to otherwise nonconscious aspects of mind, ranging from methods to aid recall of unconscious material in cognitive psychology and psychotherapeutic practice, close attention to the phenomenology of otherwise preconscious mental operations (Varela & Shear, 1999), meditative practices in Yoga and so on.

[26] Due to lack of available space I discuss the notion of 'preconscious free will', introduced in TA, in a later issue of *JCS* along with commentaries by Libet, Mangan, and Claxton. It is interesting to note, however, that **Gray**, and **Chrisley & Sloman** wholeheartedly agree that free will is preconscious as well as conscious, in spite of there being other aspects of my analysis with which they disagree.

[27] Although, following Rao, I have presented the Eastern view as idealist, it is important to note that there are as many differences in Eastern philosophy about these basic issues as there are in Western thought. The combined material and conscious nature of the thing-itself is well recognised, for example, in major, modern interpretations of Vedanta such as that of Aurobindo.

References

Arbuthnott, K.D. (1995), 'Inhibitory mechanisms in cognition: Phenomena and models', *Cahiers de Psychologie Cognitive*, **14** (1), pp. 3–45.

Baars, B.J., Banks, W.P. and Newman, J.B. (ed. 2002), *Essential Sources in the Scientific Study of Consciousness* (Cambridge, MA: MIT Press; in press).

Chalmers, A.F. (1992), *What is this Thing Called Science?* (Milton Keynes: Open University Press).

Chalmers, D.J. (1996), *The Conscious Mind* (New York: Oxford University Press).

John, E.R. (2002), 'The neuropsychology of consciousness', *Brain Res Brain Res Rev*, **39**, pp. 1–28.

Kim, J. (1999), *Mind in a Physical World* (Cambridge, MA: MIT Press).

Libet, B. (2003), 'Can conscious experience affect brain activity? *Journal of Consciousness Studies* (in press).

McFadden, J. (2002a), 'Synchronous firing and its influence on the brain's electromagnetic field: Evidence for an electromagnetic theory of consciousness', *Journal of Consciousness Studies*, **9** (4), pp. 23-50.

McFadden, J. (2002b), 'The conscious electromagnetic information (Cemi) field theory: The hard problem made easy?', *Journal of Consciousness Studies*, **9** (8), pp. 45–60.

Melzack, R. (1987), 'The short-form McGill Pain Questionnaire', *Pain*, **30**, pp. 191–97.

Metzinger, T. (ed. 2000), *Neural Correlates of Consciousness* (Cambridge, MA: MIT Press.

Miller, G. A. (1956), 'The magical number seven, plus or minus two: some limits of our capacity for processing information', *Psych Review*, **63**, pp. 81–97.

Perruchet & Vinter (2003), 'The self-organizing consciousness', *Behavioral and Brain Sciences* (in press).

Pockett, S. (2002), 'Difficulties with the electromagnetic field theory of consciousness', *Journal of Consciousness Studies*, **9** (4), pp. 51–6.

Rakover, S.S. (1992), 'Outflanking the body–mind problem: Scientific progress in the history of psychology', *Journal for the Theory of Social Behavior*, **22**, pp. 145–73.

Searle, J. (1990), 'Consciousness, explanatory inversion and cognitive science', *Behavioral and Brain Sciences*, **13** (4), pp. 585–642.

Thomson, E. (ed. 2001), *Between Ourselves: Second-Person Issues in the Study of Consciousness* (Exeter: Imprint Academic).

Varela, F. and Shear, J. (ed. 1999), *The View from Within: First person approaches to the study of consciousness* (Exeter: Imprint Academic).

Velmans, M. (1990a), 'Is the mind conscious, functional, or both?', *Behavioral and Brain Sciences*, **13**, pp. 629–30.

Velmans, M. (1990b), 'Consciousness, brain, and the physical world', *Philosophical Psychology*, **3**, pp. 77–99.

Velmans, M. (1991), 'Is human information processing conscious?', *Behavioral and Brain Sciences*, **14** (4), pp. 651–701.

Velmans, M. (1999), 'Intersubjective science', *Journal of Consciousness Studies*, **6** (2/3), pp. 299–306.

Velmans, M. (1995), 'The relation of consciousness to the material world', *Journal of Consciousness Studies*, **2** (3), pp. 200–19.

Velmans, M. (2000), *Understanding Consciousness* (London: Routledge/Psychology Press).

Velmans, M. (2001), 'Heterophenomenogy versus critical phenomenology: a dialogue with Dan Dennett', http://cogprints.ecs.soton.ac.uk/archive/00001795/index.html

Contributors

Max Velmans
Department of Psychology, Goldsmith's College
New Cross, London SE14 6NW, UK

Ron Chrisley
School of Computer Science, University of Birmingham
Birmingham B15 2TT, UK

Todd E. Feinberg
Beth Israel Medical Center
Fierman Hall, 9th Floor, 317 East 17th Street, New York, NY 10003, USA

Robert Van Gulick
Department of Philosophy, 541 HL, Syracuse University
Syracuse, NY 13244-1170, USA

Jeffrey Gray
Institute of Psychiatry
De Crespigny Park, Denmark Hill, London SE5 8AF, UK

John F. Kihlstrom
Department of Psychology, MC 1650, University of California, Berkeley
Tolman Hall 3210, Berkeley, CA 94720-1650, USA

Sam S. Rakover
Department of Psychology, Haifa University
Haifa 31905, Israel

K. Ramakrishna Rao
Department of Physiology, All India Institute of Medical Sciences,
Ansarinagar, New Delhi 110 029, India

Department of Psychology, University of North Carolina
CB #3270, Davie Hall, Chapel Hill, NC 27510, USA

Aaron Sloman
School of Computer Science, University of Birmingham
Birmingham B15 2TT, UK

Steve Torrance
School of Cognitive and Computing Sciences
University of Sussex, Falmer, Brighton BN1 9QH, UK